"I am thrilled to see this publicati⟨...⟩ only is Mark uniquely equipped to w⟨...⟩ the need for a biblically based defense of the faith is stronger now than it has been in quite a while. Thankfully, Mark's book is both biblically and theologically rooted, as well as accessible to a wide range of readers. I hope this book will make its way into numerous evangelical churches and will spur Christians on confidently to defend the faith that the Lord has so graciously given to his people."

— K. Scott Oliphint,
**Professor of Apologetics and Theology,
Westminster Theological Seminary, Philadelphia;
Author,** *Covenantal Apologetics* **and** *Know Why You Believe*

This book takes a biblical approach to apologetics for everyday Christians in real life conversations. Mark engages the reader with lively examples from his own experiences. This is one of the most down-to-earth, helpful books on apologetics that I have read.

— Mark D. Allen,
**Executive Director, Center for Apologetics
and Cultural Engagement, Liberty University;
Coauthor,** *Apologetics at the Cross:
An Introduction for Christian Witness*

The responsibility to be ready to give a reasoned explanation of the Christian faith often fills believers with fear. This is particularly the case now that a common recognition of Christianity has been eroded and even objective truth is questioned.

Dr. Farnham allays these fears and encourages us to engage with unbelievers from the coffee shop to the departure lounge. The worldviews of unbelievers are frequently based on ignorance of the Bible and are riddled by inherent contradictions and false assumptions. By gentle questioning people can be guided to deconstruct these commitments themselves, with the result that obstacles to the gospel will be broken down. This book would be ideal for an adult Sunday school class and should be read widely and its lessons implemented.

— **Robert Letham,**
Professor of Systematic and Historical
Theology, Union School of Theology,
Bridgend, Wales; Author, *The Holy Trinity*

Every Believer Confident allows you to listen in on Mark's coffee shop conversations as he gently helps others discern their worldview and offers a better way of seeing the world through the lens of Jesus. You will be pleasantly surprised at his approach that utilizes more listening and asking better questions than arguing or debating.

— **Jonathan Templeton,**
Church Planter in Spain

I'm not sure whether this book seeks to render every believer confident with regard to apologetics or with regard to evangelism. But it doesn't matter. Farnham understands the difference and brings the two together with such clarity as to render every believer confident in our common endeavor to be "prepared to make a defense to anyone who asks you for a reason for the hope that is in you." Marvelously clear, practical, and emboldening.

Excellent guidance for any layman who seeks to be more faithful and effective in gospel advance.

— **Fred G. Zaspel,**
Editor, Books at a Glance; Associate Professor
of Christian Theology, Southern Baptist Theological
Seminary; Pastor, Reformed Baptist Church, Franconia, PA

My new go-to-first book on Apologetics. This resource will be right by my side whenever I prepare sermons on evangelism and the foundations of what we believe. Mark accomplishes in this book exactly what he intended—to help the ordinary Christian fulfill the great commission, give an answer to those who ask about their hope, and to declare the mystery of Christ. A necessary addition to every pastor's library and a needed tool to prepare every believer. This book not only provides the knowledge we need to defend our faith, but it equips us to do it with gentleness and respect, engaging real people in real conversations.

— **Beau Eckert,**
Senior Pastor, Calvary Church, Lancaster, PA

In this book, Mark Farnham prepares his readers to evangelize the lost by employing apologetics in a biblically sound and theologically responsible manner. Using real-life examples, Mark skillfully moves apologetics from the esoteric realm of philosophical theology to the far more accessible realm of practical theology, which is where it ultimately belongs. He challenges his readers to not only understand the book's content, but to practice its principles. As an ideal pastor-teacher, Mark has made a wonderful contribution to the Church that will effectively "equip the saints for the work of the ministry." Readers will be encouraged, helped, and motivated to defend and proclaim the truth of the Gospel.

— George Coon,
**Director of Theological Education,
Knysna Hope, South Africa**

Christians will find Mark's simple, but profound approach to apologetics truly empowering. How do you answer a skeptic's question? By asking them a question! In learning how to ask better questions before offering answers, the possibility for a fruitful spiritual dialogue grows exponentially. Our world desperately needs a winsome presentation of the Gospel. Those who read this book and put its principles into practice will be able to give an answer for the hope that lies within us!

— Ray G. Jones, Jr.,
**Founding Pastor, Lighthouse Community
Baptist Church, Stonington, CT**

In contrast to a clichéd Christian response, the author challenges the reader to give a more reasonable, biblical response for defending the faith. Dr. Farnham communicates the truth in the common man's language. This book is a valuable asset for both those new to Christianity and veterans of apologetics.

Every Believer Confident is a readable, practical book that stimulates one to respond with a hunger to know more about everyday apologetics and how it can be used to bring more resilience and relevance to those dialogues that can occur in the marketplaces of life.

— Sandy Outlar,
Liaison to Christian Schools, Lancaster Bible College

Every
Bel**i**ever
Confident

Apologetics

for the

Ordinary

Christian

Mark J. Farnham

Every Believer Confident: Apologetics for the Average Christian
Copyright © 2019 by Mark Farnham

Published by Deep River Books
Sisters, Oregon
www.deepriverbooks.com

ISBN—13: 9781632695208
Library of Congress: 2019919085

Printed in the USA
2019—First Edition
28 27 26 25 24 23 22 21 20 19   10 9 8 7 6 5 4 3 2 1

Cover design by Joe Bailen, Contajus Designs

For Adrienne, on the occasion of our thirtieth wedding anniversary, June 3, 2019.

Your constant love and support throughout our years together have made this book possible.

Contents

Acknowledgments

Many people have had a hand in making this small book a reality. The pages here contain few original ideas. They are primarily a distillation of the apologetic approach of Cornelius Van Til, as taught to me by my primary apologetics professor at Westminster Theological Seminary, Scott Oliphint. In the classroom Scott exemplified to me the mind and heart of a true apologist—prepared, yet humble; erudite, yet approachable. I learned to pray listening to him pray in class.

Other Westminster professors and friends shaped my mind and heart also. Bill Edgar is a Renaissance man who helped move the dial of my cultural intelligence away from Philistinism toward urbanity, even if just a little. His understanding of cultural apologetics opened new worlds for me. His wonderful wife Barb taught me French, and we hail from the same part of Connecticut. She instructed me on French cheese and fig jam, and I savor them whenever I find them.

My friends in the Das and Kees Society—Matt, Nate, and Yannick—patiently brought this teetotaling Baptist up to speed in the world of Reformed Presbyterianism, and encouraged me that I could complete my doctorate. Our animated discussions helped sharpen my critical thinking and debate skills in a context of camaraderie. Dr. Anees Zaka introduced me to the world of engagement with other religions, and his boldness and tireless efforts to evangelize inspire me.

Early drafts of this work were refined by the insights of young theologians and former students, such as Jeff Mindler, Andrew Keenan, and my Apologetics classes at Lancaster Bible College. It always brings me joy to see students and alumni still actively engaging unbelievers with the gospel, using the skills they learned in class.

My son Ryan is one of the most active apologists I know, having a real gift of comfort in engaging strangers with the gospel. He exhibits the heart of Christ in his kindness when sharing the good news of Christ.

My mother-in-law Adrienne MacDonald has always encouraged me to write. She was a faithful member of my church when I served as a pastor, and early on she encouraged me to pursue writing opportunities. It has taken me many years to do that, but this book fulfills the prediction she made when I married her daughter—that someday I would write a book. It looks like I finally have.

Introduction

"What, are you some kind of religious nut?" The woman sitting next to me in the coffee shop was responding to my offer to pray for her. Karen had sat down next to me ten minutes earlier, and had sighed so loudly for the entirety of those ten minutes that I finally realized she wanted to talk. I put my book down and asked her how her day was going. She recounted her frustration with the insurance company that wouldn't cover her medical expenses. My offer to pray for her was met with a measured disdain.

"No, not a nut, but I am a Christian, and I believe that God answers prayer. Can I ask what your religious background is?"

"I am an atheist," Karen said rather abruptly.

"Oh," I replied, "you don't believe God exists?"

She thought for a moment, and then replied, "Well, I don't know if God exists or not."

"So, you're an agnostic."

"Yes, that is what I am," Karen said more confidently. Then she furrowed her brow. "Actually, I kind of believe that God is everywhere and in everything in the world."

"So, you're a pantheist," I offered.

"Yes," she said triumphantly, "I am a pantheist!" She looked relieved to have worked through her belief system and articulated it more clearly. She seemed thankful that I had helped her arrive at clarity.

"What makes you believe that God is everywhere and in everything?" I continued.

The brow furrowed again, and she answered, "That's a good question. I don't really know!"

Thus began a conversation that lasted more than two hours. All I did for most of that time was ask questions that forced Karen to examine the basis for her beliefs, while weaving the Christian gospel into the conversation.

About fifteen minutes into the conversation a man came over with a cup of coffee and sat down next to her. He joined the conversation and began raising some objections to the Christian worldview I was presenting to Karen.

After a while I stopped and asked them, "Are you together?" Karen turned and looked at Bill and said, "No, I don't know who he is."

Bill looked at me and said, "No, I don't know her, but I heard your conversation and wanted to hear what you were saying and ask my own questions."

Bill had grown up in a cult, he told me, and had rejected the Christian faith as a result, without realizing that what he was rejecting was not Christianity at all. As I questioned their beliefs and pressed them on the implications of their worldviews, their confidence began to crumble. They began to realize that much of what they believed was unsupported and contradictory. The objections they raised against the Christian faith were mostly misunderstandings of what the Bible actually teaches.

After more than two hours, Bill stood to leave, then said to me, "I don't even know what I believe anymore. You took away everything I trusted. How do you even know anything?" His entire system of unbelief had been dismantled by the questions I had been asking him and the good news of Jesus I had been presenting as a contrast.

As our conversation neared the end, I had presented the gospel clearly and challenged them to read the Gospel of John. They both agreed to do so and went their separate ways. I had fervently prayed internally that they would be ready to repent and believe in Christ right then and there, but it was obvious that they weren't ready quite yet. It was obvious, however, that neither had confidence anymore in what they had believed just a few hours earlier.

I, on the other hand, had never felt such confidence in my faith as I experienced at that moment. I was literally shaking with excitement during the last hour of our conversation, as I saw the power of the Christian faith dismantle the previously confident worldviews of Bill and Karen. I had just begun studying apologetics at Westminster Theological Seminary a few months earlier and was intensely interested in discovering if what I was learning truly worked in encounters with unbelievers.

And it did! The power of the approach I was learning rendered the unbelief of my conversation partners weak and ineffective. It allowed me to winsomely present the gospel in a way that was powerful and convincing. It was the start of a new commitment to reach lost people with the gospel of Jesus Christ. And it has been repeated countless times in the twelve years since that day.

My Story

I was not born into a Christian home, but when I was seven years old my mother came to Christ after a long search for the truth. Her transformation was radical, and it deeply impacted my life. At the age of nine I was led to Christ by Mrs. Pepper during vacation Bible school at Nepaug Congregational Church in northwestern Connecticut. When I was in fifth grade my parents put my sisters and me in Christian school. By ninth grade I was involved in S.W.A.T.—Soul-Winning Active Teens. I was trained to evangelize on the streets of West Hartford, mostly by handing out tracts and asking people to read them. It was my earliest experience of trying to share the gospel with the lost.

At the same time, however, my conservative school and church instilled within me a fear of unbelievers. Whether they intended this or not, I began to believe that I should not have relationships with non-Christians unless I was actively seeking to evangelize them. My friendships with neighborhood pals faded, and I began to avoid anyone I didn't know outside my Christian bubble unless I had a gospel tract handy. I remained active in evangelism, but found it frustrating and ineffective. I began to wonder how I would answer those who might ask questions. I was trained primarily to reach liberal Protestants and Catholics who already believed in God and the Bible, but placed their confidence in good works, rather than the free gift of the gospel.

As the years passed and I went to Bible college and seminary, I continued to occasionally attempt to evangelize, but my expectation was always that there would be little or no response to the gospel tract I offered. The problem was not the gospel tract (usually), but the fact that I had never been taught how to engage unbelievers in conversation. I did not know how to tell people I was a Christian without a sense of embarrassment (would they think I was a religious fanatic?) and fear that they would ask me a question I could not answer.

When I became a pastor in 1995 in New London, CT, I was determined to be the evangelist I always desired to be. My young family moved into the parsonage on Blydenburg Avenue and I discovered almost immediately that my next-door neighbor was a professor, and a leading expert on Søren Kierkegaard. My determination to witness to my neighbors within the first month deflated like a leaky balloon. Instead, my determination to avoid my neighbor grew.

Looking back now, I can see that I was terrified of being asked a question I couldn't answer or encountering a belief system about which I knew little. I knew (so I thought) that I could engage Catholics and liberal Protestants, but the thought of dealing with a skeptic or someone of another religion was too scary to consider.

I began to read Ravi Zacharias and other apologists, and would travel to their conferences whenever they were within 150 miles of my church. These resources helped immensely with the facts of Christianity and other belief systems, but I still struggled to know how to talk with people I met. I was growing in my knowledge but didn't know how to use that knowledge in real conversations.

I still had so many questions that I couldn't articulate. I wasn't sure that the Christian faith could answer every objection raised against it. I didn't know what to say if someone asked me to prove God's existence. I was confused about how to prove the claims of the Christian faith. Later I would come to understand that I was wrestling with questions of epistemology (how we know what we know) and metaphysics (the nature of God and reality). These are the most fundamental questions of life and experience, something that philosophers and theologians have contemplated for thousands of years.

It wasn't until a few years later that I would have my questions answered. By this time, I had completed a postgraduate degree in New Testament at Gordon-Conwell Theological Seminary, left the pastorate, and was teaching systematic theology at a seminary. I began to look for a doctoral program in the Philadelphia area and settled on Westminster Theological Seminary. I initially pursued a degree in New Testament, but sensed God was steering me away from that field. I decided to audit a master's level class in apologetics.

Since I'd had an interest in the topic for a few years, I thought the class might fill in some gaps in my knowledge. By the second week of class, lights began to come on in my brain. By the fourth week, those foundational questions were being answered left and right. By the sixth week, I decided to change my doctoral focus to apologetics, and I have never looked back.

After the first semester of doctoral studies in apologetics, I knew I had found my purpose in life. What I was learning was so thrilling, so soul-satisfying that I would lie awake at night after class and feel energized by the eternal truths I had learned that day. I struggled to fall asleep as I mulled over in my mind the glorious answers to the questions of humanity and my own heart. I wanted to jump out of bed and shout "Hallelujah!" for the wisdom and glory and light brought to us by our Savior, Jesus Christ.

This thrill has never left me. Even today as I write this, I marvel at the ability of the gospel of Jesus Christ to silence the so-called wisdom of our day to solve the world's problems, provide meaning and purpose, and to reconcile the individual to God (1 Cor. 1:18–21). I have seen the emptiness of the "answers" offered by skeptics and religious leaders alike, and the contrasting true wisdom found in the good news of Jesus. I continue to be delighted and amazed at the way the risen Christ continues to answer all the questions of humanity and all the puzzles of philosophy. My hope in this book is that you, too, will experience this same thrill.

The Purpose of This Book

There are countless good books on apologetics. This was not always so. In the last twenty years, however, books on apologetics have flown off the presses by the hundreds. There has been a newfound interest in apologetics, driven by a number of factors which will be mentioned in Chapter 1. One of the challenges for Christians interested in apologetics, however, is finding books at their level of interest and education. A large number of resources require or assume a fair amount of familiarity with philosophy or science. These are valuable and provide depth to our efforts to reach those unbelievers who stumble over philosophical and scientific objections.

Nevertheless, most Christians will not learn philosophy or science. They do not have the resources of time, money, interest, or ability to pursue a degree in one of these areas. They are not pastors, professors, or scholars. They simply want to reach their unbelieving neighbors, friends, coworkers, family, and classmates.

You may be this kind of person. You may have a burden for the lost, and have a desire to learn to defend your faith, but you can't see yourself becoming a philosopher or scientist to do so. I have good news: You don't have to!

The requirement for being a good evangelist or apologist does not include obtaining an academic degree or reading obscure texts. Jesus never commanded his disciples to go to Athens to learn at the feet of the philosophers in order to reach the world. While knowing a little about philosophy, science, and other fields of study may help, they are not necessary. The average Christian can become a skilled and effective evangelist without becoming a student of philosophy. The average Christian can learn to defend the Christian faith, share the gospel, shake the unbelief of non-Christians, present the Christian worldview, and lead people to saving faith in Jesus Christ.

That is what this book is all about—giving ordinary Christians the confidence and equipment to fulfill the Great Commission (Matt. 28:19–20), give an answer to those who question them (1 Pet. 3:15–16), and declare the mystery of Christ (Col. 4:3–4). If you consider yourself an ordinary Christian, this book is for you!

Chapter One

Understanding Apologetics

The term "apologetics" was, at one time, only rarely heard in Christian churches. Despite the widespread popularity of apologists such as C. S. Lewis and Francis Schaeffer in the 1960s and '70s and Josh McDowell in the '80s and '90s, the vast majority of evangelical Christians in America today are completely unfamiliar with the discipline of apologetics. I still regularly meet Christians who have no idea what the word means.

What is worse is that they are also unfamiliar with the concept of being prepared to give an answer to whomever might challenge their Christian commitments. They neither know how to defend their faith nor share it effectively. Many believers live with a quiet fear regarding challenges to the Christian faith. They hold firmly to the Bible, but don't want to have to think hard about *why* they believe it. As a result, many Christians avoid conversations with non-Christians about anything spiritual, since they have no confidence that they could provide answers if asked.

Yet thinking about our faith and knowing it well enough to defend it are exactly what we are commanded to do in 1 Peter 3:15–16. Here we are each commanded to prepare ourselves to give an answer, or defense, when our faith is challenged. This is a significant part of evangelism, as discussions about the gospel rarely occur without some objections being raised by the unbeliever. Additionally, this duty is for every Christian, not just for pastors or scholars. This is the missing element in many churches' evangelism strategy. The average church member feels ill-equipped to know what to say when confronted with any of the myriad attacks on the faith.

At the same time, we now live in a time where apologetics is everywhere. The last twenty years has seen an explosion of good books, websites, and resources to help Christians defend the faith in an increasingly hostile world. The advent of YouTube has made available thousands of debates and lectures on apologetics. This is a positive blessing to the body of Christ. Christians have more resources now to help them than at any other time in history.

Yet the resources available to help ordinary Christians in their encounters with unbelievers are thin. Because many apologetics materials are geared for those with an academic bent, they are only of limited value for the average Christian. Too much philosophical language, or too much theory without practical application, renders some of these tools ineffective for most.

The purpose of this book is to help ordinary Christians know, appreciate, firmly grasp, proclaim, and defend the gospel. Its ultimate goal is to strengthen the faith of Christians, so they can confidently and effectively persuade unbelievers to believe in Jesus Christ. While some of the lessons dip into philosophy, science, logic, and other disciplines, discussion is kept at a level where most people without advanced degrees can grasp and practice the principles. Its ultimate goal is to help believers lead souls to Christ.

Definitions

First Peter 3:15–16 tells us that every Christian is to be prepared to give an answer or "make a defense" when his faith is challenged. Apologetics, then, concerns the defense of the Christian faith against all forms of unbelief. The word "apologetics" comes from the Greek word *apologia* in verse 15. This is a legal term, meaning a defense against an accusation in a court of law.

One Greek lexicon gives the range of meaning of this word: "to give an answer," "to clear oneself of charges," "to defend oneself in a court of law," "to speak on behalf of oneself or of others against accusations presumed to be false."[1] In this context, when the Christian faith is falsely accused ("the Bible has errors" or "Jesus never rose from the dead"), the Christian is to give an answer that shows the accusation to be false.

Cornelius Van Til, professor of apologetics at Westminster Theological Seminary in the twentieth century and pioneer in the field, gave this simple definition: "Apologetics is the vindication of the Christian philosophy of life against the various forms of the non-Christian philosophy of life."[2] This definition shows that a study of apologetics must include every kind of objection that may be raised up against the truth of Christianity.

A more recent definition includes the importance of showing the rationality and beauty of the Christian faith. William Edgar defines apologetics as "the art of persuasion, the discipline which considers ways to commend and defend the living God to those without faith."[3] The goal of defending the faith is to persuade the unbeliever that Jesus is the Messiah, and that the unbeliever is in need of salvation. While defending the faith, however, we also ought to be *commending* it— that is, showing how the Christian faith answers the deepest needs of the human condition and makes sense of the world.

Now that we have defined apologetics, let's look into the Scriptures and see what they have to say about the act of defending the faith.

The Relationship between Apologetics and Evangelism

The goal of evangelism is to lead a person to the saving knowledge of Jesus Christ. The goal of apologetics should be the same. So what is the difference between the two? In summary, apologetics is a distinct but inseparable part of evangelism.

First, evangelism is concerned with the presentation of the gospel, and the methods used to do so. Apologetics is concerned with answering objections to the gospel, clearing away intellectual obstacles, and commending the Christian faith as the only legitimate answer to man's predicament.

Think of an all-wheel-drive car. Usually the front tires do all the work, but when they begin to slip, the rear wheels kick into action and stabilize the car. When you are proclaiming the good news of Jesus Christ, you are evangelizing. However, when someone raises objections against the Christian faith, apologetics provides answers to their challenges so that you can return to evangelizing.

Second, apologetics is just as important for Christians as it is for unbelievers. It is not only for evangelism; it is also critical to strengthening the faith of believers, grounding them more deeply in doctrine, and answering their doubts. The end result of apologetics in the church is an increased confidence in the truth, power, and reliability of the gospel, the Scriptures, and the body of Christian doctrine that comprises our faith. The lack of knowledge of apologetics is the primary reason many churches have ceased to be effective in their evangelistic efforts. If Christians doubt their own faith, or don't know it very well, they will never share it with others.

Finally, apologetics and evangelism, though distinct, are inseparable. Evangelism without apologetics is limited to monologue with unbelievers. Apologetics without evangelism is merely an intellectual exercise. They are designed to be complementary. To simply talk to an unbeliever until they interrupt you is not biblical evangelism. Evangelism should be a dialogue wherein you take the time to understand his worldview and why he does not believe in Christ, and then give answers that reveal the truth of Christianity. By keeping the focus of apologetics on winning the lost to salvation (and not something like "proving God exists"), apologetics remains in its rightful place as a partner to evangelism.

The question of the goal of apologetics leads to a discussion of the various approaches to apologetics.

Approaches to Apologetics

There are several different types or approaches of apologetics. Each contributes in different ways to the defense of the Christian faith.

Evidentialism

The most well-known approach is often called *evidentialism*. Evidentialism seeks to develop and counter challenges to the

Christian faith with detailed facts from a number of disciplines, including history, science, and philosophy. For example, when the historical reliability of the Gospels is challenged, evidential apologists study the details of the Greek text, historical events, cultural practices, geography, archaeology, interaction with Roman history, and more to establish what Matthew, Mark, Luke and John report. This tends to produce a rich and vast body of material that strengthens the case for the truth of Christianity.

How we understand the concept of *evidence* is important. Some people mistakenly believe we can "prove" the Christian faith by presenting historical, cultural, and archaeological facts. They believe that if we present enough evidence, or the right kinds of evidence, then the unbeliever *must* believe. They hope that the skeptic will be *compelled* to believe in Christ and will have no ability to resist the truth. While it is true that some Christians describe their salvation this way, such testimonies are experiential descriptions of how they felt at the moment of realization of the truth of the gospel. In reality, as we will see later, such an experience comes at the end of the Holy Spirit convicting them of sin and drawing them to Christ. God uses evidences in that process, but it is not the presentation of evidences alone that compels them to believe.

So, rather than provide irresistible and compelling proof, evidences supplement the good news of Jesus Christ as it works on the human heart. When someone sees all the historical, scientific, and philosophical truth that corroborates the message of the gospel, those evidences can confirm the truth in their hearts. This is the value of evidence. The most well-known advocates of evidentialism include Josh McDowell, Lee Strobel, and J. Warner Wallace.

Cumulative Case Apologetics

Also known as "best-explanation" apologetics, cumulative case apologetics (CCA) seeks to present a case for the Christian faith by taking all the lines of evidence from evidentialism and combining them to show that Christianity makes better sense of life in this world than other worldviews. CCA does not seek to present the Christian faith as the *only* way to answer the questions of the human condition, but merely the *best* way. What we mean by the human condition includes the place of human beings in the universe, the nature of right and wrong, free will, and the universal desire for purpose.

One well-known example of CCA is the work of C. S. Lewis (although Lewis exhibited other approaches as well). Lewis often piled up various arguments for Christianity and argued that it best described the reality of the situation. CCA highlights the explanatory power of the Christian faith to answer questions such as how there can be so much evil in the world, but also so much good. Every worldview has to be able to account for that, and advocates of CCA make compelling arguments for the Christian faith as the best explanation.

Minimal Facts Apologetics

Minimal facts apologetics (MFA) surveys the conclusions of a wide variety of experts in a particular discipline and summarizes their agreement, that is, the most basic facts that all or most agree upon. MFA then uses this agreement as a base upon which to build further arguments for the truth of Christianity. For example, when it comes to the death and resurrection of Jesus, almost no historian doubts the existence of Jesus. This includes both Christian and non-Christian historians. In addition, almost no historian doubts that Jesus was crucified by the Romans under the rule of Pontius Pilate in Jerusalem. Further, a strong majority of historians believe that Jesus' tomb was empty after three days.

MFA proceeds to argue that if everyone can agree upon these facts, then by using the same historical criteria we can rationally believe that the entire story of Jesus is true. This includes the resurrection and the claims of Jesus to be God incarnate and the Savior of the world. MFA essentially rides the scholarly consensus as far as it will go, and then shows that it ought to go farther and accept the Bible's teaching completely. Gary Habermas and Michael Licona are representatives of this approach.

Going Further

Each of these approaches has yielded powerful arguments for the Christian faith. The fruit of their research can be found in dozens of original works that have strengthened our confidence in the truth of Scripture. As apologetic methods, however, they are insufficient. On their own, they lack a methodology for effectively engaging unbelievers in the kind of gospel conversations that draw them into confrontation with the gospel demands of repentance and belief. What they lack is an approach that moves beyond the stating of facts to engaging the heart of someone who does not believe.

Although they contribute great evidences that strengthen the case for the Christian faith, these approaches start with an insufficient theological basis. Those who advocate them sometimes assume that logic and rationality are universally agreed upon (they are not), and that unbelievers will automatically accept the truth if it is clearly shown to them. Yet if the biblical description of the unsaved mind is true, no one is genuinely seeking God (Rom. 3:11) unless God draws him (Jn. 6:44). A biblical understanding of conversion, therefore, must begin with God's drawing of the sinner to make the gospel clear.

A few years ago, I was talking with a leader of a well-known apologetics ministry that works from an evidentialist approach. In order to clarify for both of us the difference between our approaches, I asked him how he goes about talking with unbelievers.

"I approach the person and ask him, 'If I can prove to you that God exists, will you believe in him?'" he explained.

I was somewhat surprised at this approach, so I asked him, "What if the person says no?"

"Then I move on to someone else," he replied.

I was flabbergasted. Given the Bible's description of the unbeliever's state of rebellion against God, opposition to the truth, and intellectual darkness, I don't expect conversations with unbelievers to be so formulaic. First, I was skeptical that "proving" God's existence would be convincing to most people. I used to try to do so in my evangelism efforts, using logic and philosophy, and found that there were more objections that could be raised than I could handle without a degree in philosophy. I have also seen skeptics flat-out refuse any argument or evidence as insufficient, no matter how coherently the case was presented.

Second, I was surprised that this apologist's tactic was so uniform. Not everyone is wrestling with the existence of God; and even if they are, it may not be the most pressing issue in their unbelief. Rather than addressing all unbelievers in the same way, there is an approach that is more responsive to the individual and his particular reason for nonbelief.

Presuppositionalism

The term *presuppositional* is derived from the word "presupposition," which refers to a basic heart commitment, or a precondition for knowledge. While many presuppositionalists prefer other names for their approach, such as *covenantal* or *transcendental*,[4] the name *presuppositional* is the most widely used. Unfortunately, as New Testament scholar Darrell Bock notes, some use this term to describe an approach that answers every objection with "The Bible tells me so." Such an inadequate approach is actually more properly called *fideism,* which rejects the idea that any rational justification for our beliefs must be given. Fideism is clearly flawed because it contradicts the clear command in 1 Peter 3:15–16 to be prepared to give an answer to those who ask us for the reasons for our faith. A true presuppositionalism, on the other hand, seeks to get to the heart of the unbeliever's challenge—to reveal its irrationality before presenting the truth of the Christian faith in all its glory and true rationality.

A presupposition is a belief that serves as a foundation for all other beliefs. For the Christian, the triune God and his revelation serve as the foundational beliefs. Unbelievers often have never considered what their most basic heart commitment is, and therefore, their foundational beliefs are unexamined. For example, they often believe that certain actions are right and good, and certain actions are wrong or evil. When pressed to tell *why* certain actions are good or evil, they often cannot provide an answer.

Presuppositions, therefore, are very important, and everyone has them. The presuppositional approach to apologetics begins with biblical truth and seeks to get at the heart of the unbeliever's rejection of the gospel. What follows are some of the basic tenets of presuppositionalism.

First, God has revealed himself, and therefore every person knows him (Rom. 1:18–21). While the evidentialist says that every person has the *capacity* to know God, the presuppositionalist says, along with Romans 1, that every person does indeed know God. The believer knows God in a relationship of grace, and the unbeliever knows God in a relationship of wrath. Because unbelievers know God, they are without excuse. Therefore, when I am sharing the truth of the Christian faith, I am speaking of a God who is already known by the unbeliever. This will be explored further in Chapter 4.

Second, the Bible attests to its own authority. Because there is no authority higher than God, his Word is the highest court of appeals for any question of truth. We call this the *self-attesting authority of Scripture*. Most other systems of belief place reason as the highest authority or test of truth. While reason is a God-given capacity, it is not an authority. Rather, reason is a tool we use to know and understand the truth. Reason helps us to clarify our beliefs and avoid contradiction in our theology, but it does not stand over Scripture to judge what is "reasonable."

Only the Christian worldview can adequately explain all aspects of the human experience in a way that is rational and that provides meaning. The reason is that this is God's world, and his description of our origin, purpose, and destiny—as well as what is wrong with this world—is the only one that works. Non-Christian worldviews and belief systems face the challenge of trying to explain God's world on their own distorted terms, and must necessarily be wrong in important ways, because only

God describes this world correctly. Because they do not accept the authority of Scripture, they oppose Christianity with their partial truths.

This book lays out a basic and practical presuppositional approach for apologetics. It does not deny the importance of evidence but begins with these Christian presuppositions. When encountering unbelief of any kind, this approach challenges the unbeliever's presuppositions to show that they cannot rationally explain life and existence. Evidences are brought into the conversation *after* her presuppositions are acknowledged. By establishing this first, you force her to accept the logical implications of her presuppositions. This prevents her from denying the evidences you offer later in the discussion, because if she has already agreed to what makes an idea rational or historical, to deny the implications is to be irrational.

For example, some who reject Christianity do so because they do not believe there is adequate historical support for the life and ministry of Jesus as recorded in the Gospels. Unless you begin by establishing how we know anything in the past, the unbeliever can deny that the biblical history is accurate. However, if you both agree that knowledge of the past is possible, and that we must rely on eyewitness accounts by reliable individuals carefully recorded and preserved to know the past, then it is relatively easy to demonstrate that the Gospels are trustworthy. If she tries to deny this after you have established the way history works, she shows herself to be self-contradictory by rejecting documents which meet the standard of reliable history.

Such a conversation may look like this:

> Christian: Can I tell you about Jesus and why he came to save us?

Skeptic: Save your breath. I don't believe that we can really know who Jesus was or what he said.

C: Really? Why not?

S: Because the Bible was written so long ago that we can't expect that the original message survived. As a result, we don't even know if Jesus existed, or if anything written about him is true.

C: Do you believe we can know the truth about anything in the past? Or can we only believe what we see presently?

S: Of course we can believe in the past! We have pictures and records of people and events. We can know some things that happened.

C: But surely some of what people claim to have happened in the past is unreliable, like George Washington chopping down the cherry tree. How do historians know if the account is true or not?

S: I suppose that it comes down to reliable testimony, artifacts, archaeology, written records, and things like that. When they corroborate the written accounts, we can believe they really happened.

C: Yes! We have to trust these accounts if they demonstrate careful reporting and are confirmed by other known historical facts. What do you find lacking in the gospel accounts of Jesus?

S: Well, I don't know specifics because I've never read the Bible, but didn't his followers write the accounts? How can we believe they weren't exaggerating or making up miracles? They believed in Jesus, so their testimony doesn't count.

C: Everyone who writes a biography about another person believes that person existed, otherwise they wouldn't write the story, so that can't count against the gospel writers. In addition, they were careful to question eyewitnesses, research, and report known facts. Look at Luke's Gospel. It begins with Luke telling his readers that he researched carefully all the facts in the book. That sounds like a reliable testimony to me. It was clearly not a book full of legends and made-up stories. Hundreds of facts mentioned in the Gospels have been verified by history, geography, archaeology, and other fields. I would think that would qualify as reliable as much as any other ancient account.

S: I didn't know that. I thought the New Testament was full of mythical accounts of Jesus that couldn't be verified in any way.

C: Let me encourage you to read the Gospels to see who Jesus really is and what he said about himself.

While this imaginary conversation is simplistic, it demonstrates the need to expose the presuppositions of your conversation partner before presenting evidence for the Christian faith. We want to make sure we establish the standard for what is rational, historical, and ethical before we argue that the Christian faith meets those standards. Once we do this, the unbeliever has a choice between accepting the truth of Christianity or being irrational. This approach will be explained throughout the book in greater detail—so if the concept is still unclear, be patient and read on.

Conclusion

In the next few chapters we will unpack the main ideas behind the presuppositional approach, explain them in detail, and show how they work in real-life apologetic encounters. These lessons combine a number of different aspects of apologetics, such as worldview, logic, theology, evangelism, and world religions. These all constitute pieces of a puzzle that won't fully make sense or fit together until toward the end of the book. It is important, then, to be patient with the process. Learning apologetics is very much like learning a language, which starts slowly with basics and moves into more complicated aspects. Throughout the entire process, the student must master elements of the language that won't be put into use fully until he becomes conversant in the language.

In the same way, becoming a well-trained apologist requires mastering certain theological concepts and philosophical ideas that kick into gear when the time is right. The key is for us to retrain our minds to think in a distinctly Christian way. This constitutes a major shift in the thinking of many Christians, because we don't often realize how secularized our thinking has become. We have lost confidence in the Word of God because of the relentless cultural and intellectual assaults against our faith from all corners.

When we take a step back, however, and immerse ourselves again in the Scriptures, we find our confidence restored and our strength renewed. We also find a number of assumptions and ideologies that we must shake off to reinstate a Christian mind. We need to be constantly renewing our minds so they will be transformed (Rom. 12:2). The way we do this is to behold the glory of the Lord in his Word (2 Cor. 3:18). When we develop a thoroughly Christian mind, defending the faith becomes more natural and powerful.

In the next chapter we will look at the biblical warrant for apologetics. From Genesis to Revelation, God is defending his glory as it is assaulted by Satan and those who follow him. In every case, God rises to defend his glory; and in the process, he assures us that the good news of his saving power is heard.

Chapter Two

The Biblical Warrant
for Apologetics

Quite often, when I explain to other believers what I do in my apologetics conferences, I get either blank stares (because they don't know what apologetics is) or a smirking, knowing look because they believe that I have succumbed to philosophy and think that I have lost confidence in the Scriptures. Even though many are frustrated with evangelism and their attempts to reach the unbelievers in their lives, they don't seem to realize that apologetics offers the resources they need to become more effective. And when I show them the biblical warrant for defending the faith, many express surprise that they never noticed these truths in their Bible reading.

It is important for believers to see clearly that defending the truth and glory of God is a biblical idea. Apologetics is sometimes mistaken for a philosophical intrusion into Christianity, or an ill-advised invention to counter Enlightenment modernism. Even luminaries such as British Baptist pastor Charles Spurgeon and Prime Minister of Netherlands, Abraham Kuyper, made disparaging remarks about apologetics.

Spurgeon's famous jibe is well-known: "There is no need for you to defend a lion when he is being attacked. All you need to do is to open the gate and let him out." Many use this oft-repeated line to argue that we don't need apologetics. In addition to being the Prime Minister, Kuyper was a theologian, journalist, and statesman, and was the founder of the Free University of Amsterdam at the beginning of the twentieth century. He wrote, "Apologetics has advanced us not one single step. Apologists have invariably begun by abandoning the assailed breastwork, in order to entrench themselves cowardly in a ravelin [fortification] behind it."

Both of these quotes are often taken out of context, however. Spurgeon was talking about the need to proclaim the Word of God, instead of endlessly arguing about it. His point was that proclaiming the words of Scripture is powerful enough to win people to the truth. Likewise, Kuyper was not speaking against all apologetics, but rather against that approach that concedes unregenerate man's ability to reason objectively to the truth of the gospel, and that places reason in the place of judgment over Scripture.

A negative reaction to apologetics is unfortunately all too common. I asked a Christian college professor one time how he would answer someone who challenged the Christian faith. His response stunned me. "I wouldn't," he replied. I assumed that he misunderstood my question, so I rephrased it. "How would you defend the resurrection if someone challenged it?" His response was the same: "I wouldn't defend it. I would just state it and be done."

This might sound spiritual, but it is nothing more than a repudiation of our calling in 1 Peter 3:15–16 to prepare ourselves to give an answer. Rather than abandoning apologetics, we need to see it as a critical part of evangelism. If we abandon apologetics, we abandon evangelism. Scott Oliphint reminds us, "Apologetics is premeditated evangelism."[6] By preparing ourselves beforehand we can be ready for any opportunity that comes our way to share the gospel.

The real question, however, is whether there is a biblical precedent for defending the Christian faith, and its related themes, such as the glory of God, the truth, and the gospel. This chapter focuses on the biblical teaching about the theme of defense throughout the Old Testament, and the specific instruction about apologetics in the New Testament.

The Old Testament

The Garden of Eden (Gen. 3:9–24)

Right from the very first chapters of the Bible, we see that God set a precedent in defending his glory. In response to Adam and Eve's disobedience, God confronted the violation of his glory and the error that Satan perpetrated among those made in his image. God did this, not from a distance, but by condescending (stooping down to their level) and coming near to Adam and Eve. The adversarial nature of Satan's temptation and corruption of the garden and the first pair was matched and overcome by God's determination to restore what was ruined. In the midst of curses leveled against all involved, God promised ultimate deliverance and restoration through the seed of the woman.

The fall introduced enmity to God's world, and so God defended his glory by banning Adam and Eve from the garden. God is the defender, and he sets the example for us to defend the truth when it is challenged. God does not overlook sin or the corruption of his world. He confronts it directly through his sovereign rule over the universe, and indirectly through our witness to the truth.

The Exodus

In God's deliverance of Israel from Egypt, the primary concern was not the deliverance of Israel, but rather their deliverance in a way that showed God's power over the Egyptian gods. The exodus was an apologetic against the weakness of Egyptian deities. When God called Moses to lead the people out of Egypt, it was for the express purpose of manifesting his glory and supremacy (Exod. 3:15; 6:7; 7:3, 5; 8:18–19; 9:16; 10:1–2; 11:9).

God confronted Pharaoh, who thought that he himself was a god who held power over the Israelites. By confronting Egypt by means of the plagues, God clearly showed the world that he is the true God. His deliverance of Israel from Egypt became a testimony to the world that there is only one God to fear—Israel's God. By obeying God's call to lead Israel, even though he felt inadequate, Moses became the spokesman for God's declarations against Egypt and for the power and supremacy of the true God.

David and Goliath

When the Philistine giant cursed God and dared Israel to send him a suitable opponent, no soldier took up the challenge. But a teenage shepherd heard Goliath taunt Israel and curse God and found that he could not ignore such a threat. David's motivation was not for personal glory, nor was it to overcome "giants" in his life. What drove him to accept Goliath's challenge was his jealousy for the glory of God's name (1 Sam. 17:41–47). He wanted the whole world to know that there was a God in Israel and that the battle was the Lord's.

David's passion for God's glory enabled him to see that the physical challenge of Goliath was more than a conflict of military forces. In the ancient world, everybody believed that whichever side won the battle possessed a stronger god or gods than the losing side. Goliath taunted the Israelites because they were so weak, and this reflected on Yahweh, Israel's God. This was why David could not refrain from confronting Goliath. Silence was the equivalent of consenting that the Philistine gods were more powerful than Yahweh. David's great victory over Goliath manifested to Israelite and Philistine alike that Israel's God was the true God.

God's Declarations in Isaiah

In the later chapters of Isaiah God confronted the idolatry of Israel and reminded them that he is the only true God. He taunted the pagan gods that Israel preferred to worship, exposing them as powerless (Isa. 41:24), a delusion (41:29), and nothing more than empty wind (41:29). He stated clearly that no god existed before him, and that none will exist after him either (43:10). These gods cannot save (45:20, 46:7). Over and over, God reminded Israel that there is no other God besides him (44:6, 8; 45:5-6, 14, 18, 20–22; 46:7, 9).

Why did God go to so much trouble to discredit these false gods? He stated plainly that he refused to share his glory with any pretender (42:8). God is jealous for his glory, and he will not allow false deities to receive the glory that is due only to him. God's jealousy, unlike ours, is an appropriate response to pagan worshipers ascribing to their idols what is only true of God. Only God is worthy to be praised. Only he is the Creator and Sustainer of the World. Only he has provided genuine salvation, unlike the false deliverance promised by false gods who do not answer or save when called upon (46:7).

Summary

In the Old Testament, a pattern emerges of God confronting violations of his Word and his glory. God upholds and defends his glory, and his people are called upon to do the same. In the New Testament this pattern continues, with more specific instruction given regarding how Christians are to go about this task.

New Testament

The Primary Instruction on Apologetics (1 Peter 3:15–16)

A number of New Testament passages speak directly to the practice of apologetics. Some of these will be developed in greater depth in the chapters to come, so this section will focus exclusively on the *locus classicus* (the best known or most authoritative passage on the topic) of apologetics in the New Testament.

This is the primary passage in the New Testament laying out the responsibility of every Christian to practice apologetics. First Peter is written in the context of suffering and persecution. The audience of the book is a combination of Jewish and Gentile Christians who have been scattered by persecution and are struggling to know how to live in a hostile world. Their former place of inclusion in pagan culture before conversion has been replaced with antagonistic exclusion from society. They have been marginalized as members of society who don't count, and therefore, could be exploited.

Yet Peter calls them to live boldly and triumphantly, knowing that the opposition they face has already been doomed by the victorious resurrection of Jesus from the dead. As a result, he calls them to engage those who persecute them. Ultimately no one can harm the Christian, even though temporarily believers can and do suffer great tribulation (Jn. 16:33). Peter encourages his readers to resist the fear that results from the threats of their persecutors (3:13–14).

Rather than fear, Peter instructs them to turn the table on their persecutors when they are questioned about their faith and challenged to explain themselves. He admonishes every believer, not simply pastors or scholars, to prepare themselves for this inevitable event. The apologetic task includes several elements.

First, we are to begin with a settled assurance that Jesus is the Lord (v. 15a). Peter's first concern is for the believer's own heart. The command is a Greek word that is variously translated "sanctify," "set apart," or "consider to be holy." The idea is that the Christian must begin with both a knowledge of his faith and a confidence that it is true. Unless you believe firmly that Jesus is the true King over all the earth, that his Word is true, and that he is what every person needs most, you will not possess the confidence needed to engage unbelievers effectively.

As Peter is writing his epistle, his audience is suffering under the oppressive Roman Empire that declared that Caesar was Lord. Therefore, Peter's words stand in opposition to the political powers of the day. Regardless of what men may declare concerning their own power, only Jesus is the true Lord.

This personal declaration of the truth of Jesus must be something settled in the believer's heart. In other words, when the Word of God is fully accepted as the authoritative revelation given from God, Jesus will be held as the one and only Lord.

For many Christians in the West today, finding confidence that Jesus is the only Lord and Savior of mankind is difficult.

Since the advent of the internet and the greater awareness of other religions in the wake of 9/11, Christians in America are exposed to a bewildering array of worldviews and religions they never knew existed before. Combined with the culture's constant demand for tolerance, the average believer is hesitant to declare the exclusivity of Christ, let alone possess a strong sense of conviction about it internally.

I know what it feels like to waver on this point. For many years I struggled to believe with certainty that I could demonstrate that Jesus is the only way to be reconciled to God. It was not that I doubted it for myself, but I wasn't sure I could convincingly prove it to someone who believed differently. These two issues, believing the lordship of Christ and proving it, are two different issues. I may not be able to convince someone else, but I need to be convinced myself in order to present a compelling defense of Jesus as Lord.

Second, prepare yourself to make a defense of the faith (v. 15b). After settling Christ's lordship in their hearts, Christians are to prepare themselves for challenges to their faith leveled by unbelievers. The word translated "prepared" is used in the context of outfitting a ship for a voyage. Just as a ship's captain would carefully load a ship with food, water, sails, medicine, and other supplies before a long voyage, so a Christian ought to prepare himself for any number of challenges raised against the faith.

How does a Christian prepare? As mentioned above, the first thing a Christian must do is to learn the Christian faith thoroughly. This means knowing the Scriptures thoroughly and having a firm grasp of Christian theology. Many believers try to defend the faith without knowing what they believe. This results in an ineffective apologetic, which has to continually concede ground to unbelief. Those who are well-schooled in theology, however, find many more resources at their disposal in the apologetic task.

I regularly meet Christians who are very interested in apologetics and in engaging unbelievers with the gospel. Once we begin to talk details of their experiences, however, it becomes obvious that they barely know the Scriptures and don't have much interest in devoting time to doctrine. While the term "systematic theology" can be intimidating to the average believer, it is nothing more than an in-depth study of what God has revealed about himself and the world for the purpose of relationship with us. The problem, however, is that many Christians have a negative view of theology and attend churches where the term is rarely mentioned and less often taught. As a result, these zealous evangelists barely know the faith they are defending. At best all they can present is a bare-bones, and often distorted, version of the Christian faith.

In addition to knowing their own faith, Christians should also know as much as they reasonably can about their conversation partner's beliefs. This isn't always possible, but if you are having a second or third discussion about the Christian faith with someone, it is helpful to know at least a little about what that person believes.

Preparation requires an investment of time, effort, and sometimes money. It takes careful thought, reading, studying, and conversations to become an experienced apologist. There are many good books that contribute to the Christian's preparation, and investing money in them is an important element of being ready when the time comes. The more you devote to thoroughly knowing the Scriptures and sound doctrine, the deeper the well of resources you will draw from in your evangelism.

Third, defend the faith in a way that encourages conversation (v. 15c). Peter calls us to prepare so we can "give an answer" or "make a defense." The Greek word is *apologia*, from which we get the word "apologetics." This is a legal term that means to defend a position in a court of law against charges. Many of the objections raised against Christianity are accusations that call for an answer. All Christians should be able to defend the faith against these accusations.

An important truth should be emphasized here: *The Christian faith can stand up to any legitimate challenge raised against it.* In other words, believers do not need to fear that objections exist for which there is no answer. They do not need to worry that someone may someday discover an objection that Christianity cannot answer. Since the days of the apostles, Christians have been faced with challenges and have been developing answers.

A significant part of my own journey to confirm this for myself has been to learn enough history, philosophy, science, sociology, and other fields that I can provide answers when asked questions. Many times during this process, I would pursue various streams of anti-Christian arguments just to see if the Christian faith could provide an answer. I can say with full assurance that I have never been disappointed. Every legitimate objection raised against Christianity has a satisfying answer, both philosophically and emotionally.

While I was working on my doctorate in apologetics at Westminster Theological Seminary my doctoral cohort and I used to gather several times a month and discuss what we were learning. We would read the latest in philosophy, history, and literature, and discover together the strength of the Christian faith to provide answers to the challenges raised in these fields.

At that time several of us were taking external classes at other universities in the Philadelphia area. One of the schools was well known for its philosophy department, and through a series of conversations we decided to host a friendly debate between doctoral students and junior instructors at both schools. The evening of the meeting saw more than twenty students and onlookers gather to discuss the problem of evil and the existence of God. One of the brighter students in our group (not me!) presented a paper to the mostly atheistic doctoral students in the philosophy department at the other school. He gave a distinctly Christian answer to the problem of evil and suffering, emphasizing all the fullness and glory of the answers found in Jesus Christ (2 Cor. 4:1–6).

The respondent of the evening was the *de facto* leader of the students from the other school. He was already an instructor and recognized as the brightest of the bunch. All his fellow atheists looked eagerly at him as he prepared his retort. It never came. For almost ten minutes he shuffled his papers, hemmed and hawed, and could barely formulate more than a few sentences in response. At one point he muttered, "Well, I wasn't really prepared for that kind of argument." It was clear to everyone in the room that evening that the "irrational" Christian students of apologetics presented a sound biblical and philosophical argument for God, and the "rational" philosophy students couldn't muster much of a rejoinder.

This is not to say that unbelieving philosophers don't present scholarly and eloquent cases for unbelief. They do. But when subjected to the scrutiny of a well-trained apologist, their arguments are often exposed for the foolishness they truly are (1 Cor. 1:18–25). One needs only watch a few of Ravi Zacharias' public addresses, and the question-and-answer times that follow, to see how powerful the Scriptures are to "put to silence the ignorance of foolish people" (1 Pet. 2:16). Yet, he gives an answer in a kind and respectful manner. He treats his challengers with dignity, validating the truth in their questions while at the same time dismantling their unbelief and presenting the gospel in all its wisdom and beauty.

While the challenges we encounter may at times be hostile or antagonistic, we should never respond in kind. Peter describes the proper demeanor of the apologist—gentleness and respect. First, when engaged in conversation with an unbeliever, the Christian should speak and act in a way that is humble, approachable, and winsome. The goal is not to argue with or shame the non-Christian, but rather to help him see the light of truth. Gentleness speaks to our tone of voice, our understanding of God's love for the person, and our refusal to be aggressive or antagonistic.

This is important for several reasons. Jesus always dealt with unbelievers this way. He invited and encouraged conversation with skeptics like Nicodemus, the dishonest like Zacchaeus and Matthew, the immoral like the woman at the well, and many others. He did not simply confront them about their sin but spoke to them like human beings made in the image of God. He was kind and concerned, and these characteristics opened doors for lengthy conversations.

Once when I was teaching a seminary class on apologetics, a student enrolled in the class who was not seeking a degree. He only wanted to take the one apologetics class. As the semester proceeded, I began to understand why. He worked for a trucking company, and many of his coworkers were Muslim. He was actively studying the Qur'an, so he could argue with them and prove them wrong. He took my class because he wanted more ammunition to argue with his fellow workers. One day when I was sharing the story of my conversation with a particularly antagonistic unbeliever, he raised his hand and asked, "How did you have the patience not to just punch him right in the face?" I was stunned, thinking he was joking, but he wasn't. I reiterated that the goal of evangelism and apologetics is not to win arguments (or punch people in the face), but to winsomely show them the good news of Jesus.

Peter is encouraging a gentle demeanor in our encounters with non-Christians. Gentleness should not imply weakness, as our culture has come to understand it. Rather, gentleness suggests being *winsome*—that is, courteous, likeable, non-offensive. It implies that others *want to* have a conversation with you and are willing to listen to what you have to say. A gentle person doesn't force a conversation on you but invites you into a conversation that is nonthreatening and compelling.

Coffee shops tend to be the place I have the most apologetics conversations, since I work and spend most of my time on the campus of a Christian college. One day a man sat down next to me and began reading his book. I have found that one of the best conversation-starters is to simply ask people about the book they are reading. Abram was reading a book by New Age guru Deepak Chopra. I asked him what he was reading and what it was about. He proceeded to tell me that it was about self-actualization or becoming all you were meant to be and finding your potential. When I began to question his ideas, he stopped me and told me that he did not like to share these things with Christians, because they did not understand.

I could have pressed on and renewed my challenge, but instead I said, "OK," and returned to my studying. About ten minutes later he loudly closed his book, turned to me, and said,

"You know that thing you said about . . .", and the conversation resumed. Had I not gently given him space, he probably would not have been willing to talk further. Our conversation continued for another half-hour, and I was able to present the gospel to him once he was more open to hear it.

In addition to gentleness, Peter encourages our demeanor to be marked by the Greek word *phobos*, from which we get "phobia," or fear. This word is also translated "respect." He never explains this concept further, so it can have one of three possible meanings: First, Peter could be encouraging believers to fear God when engaging unbelievers. In other words, rather than be overcome by the fear of man, which paralyzes and silences the apologist, we should fear God, which brings boldness.

Second, the word could be referring to the fact that apologetic encounters always involve fear. This choice means that when we feel fear, we should remind ourselves that this is normal. Fear should be expected, and therefore should not deter us from continuing the conversation. Rather than running away from the situation, which we naturally do when afraid, Peter could be encouraging us to continue the conversation with the unbeliever, even in the presence of fear.

Third, Peter could be using this word in its other sense, to be "respectful." In a number of passages *phobos* has the sense of treating someone with dignity or respect (e.g., Rom. 13:7; 1 Pet. 2:18; 3:2). It means to remember that the unbeliever is made in the image of God and is loved by God, even while they are estranged from him. Jesus never demeaned anyone in his conversations with them, but rather treated them with kindness and dignity, even while he confronted their unbelief. In John 4, Jesus rejected every reason culture afforded him to treat the woman at the well with disdain. Instead he spoke to her with kindness, offering hope and redemption.

In the same way we must treat even the most antagonistic person with kindness, knowing that they are ultimately opposing God, not us. We do so to break down the barriers of hostility that have been built up against the gospel. Even when we have to engage in firm confrontation of falsehood in a person's worldview, we do so seeking to draw that person to the beauty and glory of Christ. As the old saying goes, "You draw more flies with honey than with vinegar!"

Fourth, practice regular repentance (v. 16). The final point Peter makes deals with the Christian's heart condition and lifestyle. Too many Christians today are trying to defend the Christian faith when their own lives do not in any way demonstrate an attitude of humble repentance concerning their own sin. They are quick to point out the sin of others, but their consciences are guilty with hidden sin, arrogant and self-righteous behavior, and other unconfessed sins.

Peter emphasizes that a Christian with a clear conscience is a powerful apologetic, because his life cannot be impeached by accusations of hypocrisy. Instead, when he is indicted for violating the very life-transforming gospel that he proclaims, and the charges are investigated, he is found innocent. The enemies of the gospel find they have nothing bad to say about the lives of Christians whom they oppose. So even a believer's life is a legal defense against objections to the gospel. This is important because many people reject the Christian faith for the very reason that they know professing Christians who are immoral, dishonest, or cruel and judgmental.

By living a humble and repentant life, the Christian puts to silence the foolish charges of ignorant people who oppose

Christianity for no good reason (1 Pet. 2:15). The believer can share his faith confidently, because he has nothing to hide and can invite the unbeliever to examine his life to see that there is no hypocrisy.

Conclusion

It should be clear by now that apologetics has a solid biblical basis. It is rooted in God's consistent confrontation of man's sin and unbelief, and his jealous defense of his glory in the face of false belief and idolatry. We defend the Christian faith because the glory of God is at stake. We do so as God's emissaries, shining the light of the knowledge of the glory of Christ into a world blinded by sin and darkness (2 Cor. 4:3–6)

In addition, we ought to settle the matter of Christ's lordship in our own hearts by having a thorough knowledge of Scripture and sound doctrine. This preparation will enable us to defend the truth and glory of the gospel in the face of challenges raised against it. We do so with a Christlike demeanor, combined with a life of integrity. This biblical description of apologetics will result in a powerful impact on the world. We will see a renaissance of churches full of evangelists and apologists. The church will once again stand as a shining light, piercing the darkness with the good news of the risen Christ (Lk. 11:33).

Chapter Three

The Power of Apologetics

I entered the philosophy class for the first time with some fear and trepidation. I was required to take some doctoral level classes at another institution and had chosen a class on the nineteenth-century philosopher Friedrich Nietzsche. Nietzsche is famous for his "Parable of the Madman," in which he declared "God is dead." While registering a few weeks before I thought, "Why not?" As I mentioned in the previous chapter, I wanted to see how well the Christian faith could answer the challenges of philosophy. I need not have worried.

As the professor began to wax eloquent about Nietzsche, he made a startling statement: "There are no interpretations of Nietzsche, only misinterpretations." Some students in the class murmured approval and nodded their heads knowingly. As I was already in my forties, and not intimidated by the professor as many of my twentysomething classmates were, I raised my hand and asked, "So if there are only misinterpretations of Nietzsche, then there is no way to get anything but an A in the class, since there is no correct way to interpret his work, right?" The professor smiled benignly and had I been sitting close enough, he might have patted me on the head for my naivete. He replied,

"That is clever, but there are acceptable misinterpretations and unacceptable misinterpretations, so you must get it right."

Confused? Yeah, me too. Frustrated? I was certainly exasperated at his response. But I saw right through it. This was the acceptable foolishness of philosophy in academic circles. It seemed that not many in the class acknowledged the contradiction and hypocrisy of the professor's statement. This is exactly what Paul talked about in Romans 2:15, where he tells us that unbelievers have conflicting or contradictory beliefs that they maintain to excuse their rebellion against God. Their self-contradiction accuses their conscience of irrational behavior while simultaneously defending their behavior (literally, forming an apologetic against any conviction!). This incident demonstrates that the supposed intellectual authorities of the world are not as wise as they would like to think.

God's Wisdom vs. Human Wisdom

When an opportunity arises to engage an unbeliever with the gospel, a Christian can often feel he is at a disadvantage when it comes to the authority of his message. The world considers its "wise men" to be the only authorities in a discussion—scientists, philosophers, politicians, etc. The Bible is often dismissed out of hand as an authority, and so is discounted. To appeal to it often seems to be a sure sign that an argument has no merit on its own.

In fact, however, when we compare the authority of God's Word to the so-called "wisdom" of this age, the Scriptures prove themselves to be in a different class altogether (1 Cor. 1:18–21). While these necessary and good aspects of culture can be channels for God's truth, they are often presented as autonomous authorities. "Autonomy" is a word that means "a law by itself."

In other words, when a person refuses to base his ideas or beliefs on anything outside himself, he is trying to act autonomously. He is essentially saying, "I don't need anyone to tell me what to think or do."

When human authorities, such as scientists and philosophers, declare themselves to be autonomous, they always proceed to demean the authority of God. God becomes a competitor to them, someone who is a rival to their power and authority. They may allow other human authorities to weigh in on issues, but they will not allow God to exercise his authority in a matter of truth. This explains the disdain and hostility toward the Bible, which is so common in the world. Christians may be intimidated by this disregard for God's Word, but our confidence can be restored when we remember God's authority. Apologetics is, ultimately, a battle of authorities.

God's Authority

Contrary to those who believe in an evolutionary worldview, this is God's world. God is the one who created it, rules over it, sustains it, and will bring it to an end. The way God describes the world is not just one view among many. Rather, God's words called the world into being, and only he has the wisdom and omniscience to accurately describe the world as it truly is. The Christian's authority starts with the person of God himself. The Trinity is the beginning of all authority in heaven and earth. And everything God does is authoritative and unalterable.

Nothing happens in the universe without God's sovereign guidance and control. He is the true authority in this world. First Corinthians 1:17–25 tells us that the so-called authorities of the day—the wise man, the scribe, and the debater—have been silenced by the wisdom of God. All the wisdom of the world put together cannot lead a person to the knowledge of God or anything else of significance. These authorities face several problems:

First, they have limited knowledge. Being limited and creaturely, even the best and brightest people have only a very tiny knowledge and understanding of the universe. For example, scientists know that the universe is more than 93 percent dark matter, yet they don't know what dark matter is.

Second, they have to constantly admit they were wrong. The very nature of science is such that it is constantly overturning previous claims of knowledge. What was once declared to be certain is often proven to be wrong and is replaced by still other declarations.

Even experts in the same areas disagree. Sometimes even within the same discipline experts disagree strongly with one another. Philosopher Peter van Inwagen notes that after three thousand years of philosophy, no agreement has been found among philosophers on the nature of reality. Each philosopher disagrees with the other.[7]

What does this all mean? Although these areas of study are good, useful tools to discover our world, they can never stand as final authorities on any question of truth. And when an unbeliever appeals to science or philosophy to defend his rejection of the Christian gospel, he often doesn't realize the authority to which he is appealing is not sufficient to support his arguments.

In contrast, Christians have the authority of the risen Messiah Jesus when they share the truth of Christianity. Before he ascended to heaven, Jesus reminded his disciples that all authority in heaven and earth resides in him (Matt. 28:18). In the task that Jesus gave us to make disciples, we have his authority when we go. We do not go alone when we speak to others about Jesus.

We go as ambassadors with the authority of God, to proclaim Jesus in the power of the Holy Spirit (2 Cor. 6:18–20).

Rather than base our message on human authorities, we base it on God's authority. God is the one who has commanded everyone everywhere to be saved (Acts 17:30). Since this is God's world and he has given his Son to be the ransom for sin, God has the authority both to command people to be saved, and to serve as our sufficient authority in our evangelism.

One of the implications of this is that the source of power in evangelism and apologetics is not our own but is God's. God the Holy Spirit is the active, dynamic, supernatural power behind the transformation that takes place in salvation. In the next section, we look at the roles of the Holy Spirit and prayer in apologetics.

The Holy Spirit and Prayer in Apologetics

Because apologetics is a *spiritual* endeavor more than it is a philosophical one, believers can never forget two simple truths.[8] First, the Holy Spirit is the power and ultimate persuasion behind apologetics. We dare not seek to persuade unbelievers of the truth of the gospel in our own power. Since salvation is essentially the supernatural regeneration of a person dead in sin, the Spirit must be the active power behind someone becoming saved. Human effort and persuasion cannot bring about regeneration. This means that when I share the gospel with someone, I am not trying to convert him by my own power, but rather sharing and defending the truth that he must embrace in order to be transformed by the Holy Spirit.

This is important to remember, or else we can quickly depend on our own persuasiveness and personality to evangelize. This can lead to discouragement and fear that we didn't say something exactly right, and may lead us to believe that the person's salvation is dependent upon us, when it is not. We can come to believe that it is our eloquence and ability that brings people to Christ. This often results in a focus on techniques that pressure, manipulate, or coerce unbelievers into "making a decision." However, the Bible never describes salvation as the result of making a decision. A person is saved when he repents of his sin and places his faith in Jesus.

In order for a person to repent he must first be convicted of his sin to the point that he wants to turn from it to Christ. This will not happen if the Holy Spirit is not changing his heart toward his sin. We read in Hebrews that Esau tried to the point of tears to repent but could not because the Spirit had not convicted him (Heb. 12:17). We realize, then, that while we confront unbelievers with the need to repent of sin, only the Holy Spirit can produce real repentance in the heart. Likewise, unless the Holy Spirit convinces the unbeliever that Jesus is the Son of God who is the way, the truth, and the life (Jn. 14:6), he will not turn to Jesus for salvation.

The Holy Spirit's role in salvation is mentioned throughout the New Testament. The Holy Spirit is the one who bears witness about Christ to the unbeliever (Jn. 15:26). The Holy Spirit convicts people of their sin (Jn. 16:8). The Holy Spirit fills the hearts of evangelists with boldness (Acts 4:31). The Holy Spirit makes the message of the gospel unable to be rejected honestly (Acts 6:10). The Holy Spirit directs believers to the lost, so we can see all encounters as divine appointments (Acts 8:29). The Holy Spirit may also prevent us from going to certain places or people for a time (Acts 16:6). The power of the Holy Spirit gives us hope and enables us to fulfill the ministry to which God has called us (Rom. 15:13, 19). The Holy Spirit's message is one of true wisdom in contrast to the foolishness of human wisdom (1 Cor. 2:13).

It is obvious by this list of verses that without the Holy Spirit, all our efforts to win the lost will be in vain. The Holy Spirit and prayer are the means by which closed doors and closed hearts are opened (Col. 4:2–6).

Second, prayer is the only thing that can influence people who seem cold, closed, and unwilling to discuss spiritual things. Prayer is also the means by which we remember that salvation must be a work of the Spirit. Apologetics is a spiritual battle more than it is an intellectual battle, since an unbeliever's opposition to the truth is primarily an ethical one, not an intellectual one. Prayer is the primary evidence that we are depending on God and not ourselves. Those who pray much are fully dependent. Those who pray little demonstrate self-reliance for the persuasiveness of their witness. Given this truth, our apologetic does not end when the conversation is over, for we can ask God to convict and draw them to himself.

When we pray for God to save someone, we are asking God to override their blindness to help them see the light of the knowledge of the glory of God (2 Cor. 4:6). We are asking God to stop the person from continuing in unbelief. We are asking God to show them the emptiness of life without Christ. In every version of our prayers for unbelievers we are asking God to do what we cannot. Our prayers show our reliance on the Holy Spirit's convicting work in the heart of our conversation partner.

The roles of the Holy Spirit and prayer should increase our confidence to share the gospel, because we know the power does not come from us. Our role is to simply pray and speak. God's job is to save.

This leads us into the next topic—the difference between persuasion and argument. When many people hear the word "apologetics," they think of arguing with unbelievers about the truth. For those who love arguing, this sounds fun. For the majority of Christians, however, the prospect of arguing with unbelievers about the truth of the Christian faith holds no appeal.

Persuasion vs. Argument

The good news is that apologetics is not about arguing with people in a contentious manner, but rather seeking to persuade. The good news of Jesus was never spread through quarreling, but through persuasion. Persuasion can be defined as the art of speaking to people who are indifferent or resistant to what we have to say and moving them closer to our position.[9] Returning to 1 Peter 3:15–16, we note several principles regarding persuasion in apologetics.[10]

First, apologetics is not about starting arrogant arguments with unbelievers. We are not trying to prove them wrong, humiliate them, or make ourselves feel smarter. Rather, our goal is to present a reasonable defense of the truths of the Christian faith. As Kevin DeYoung has been known to say, "We don't want people to think that we are always right, but we want them to know that the Bible is never wrong." We show how Christianity is built on rational, biblical truth that does not contradict itself, as well as on verifiable historical events. In doing this, we aim to continue the conversation until it can be focused on Jesus.

We also need to discern between arguing and being argumentative. Argument is a natural part of life, and simply denotes the way we seek to logically present ideas. Being argumentative, on the other hand, is an attitude of opposing ideas just for the sake of it, or for the love of conflict. This is the equivalent of being contentious or quarrelsome. As G. K. Chesterton quipped, "A quarrel can end a good argument. Most people today quarrel because they cannot argue."

Because apologetics involves the give-and-take of conversation, arguing your point is a natural means of persuasion. Just as Paul argued and reasoned with those to whom he shared the gospel (Acts 19:8–9; 25:8), so in seeking to persuade people of the gospel, we argue the truth of Christianity, albeit with gentleness and respect.

Second, we are not responsible to convince anyone of the truth of the gospel, simply to present it in a convincing way. As Greg Bahnsen says:

> We can offer sound reasons to the unbeliever, but we cannot make him subjectively believe those reasons. We can refute the poor argumentation of the unbeliever, but still not persuade him. We can close the mouth of the critic, but only God can open the heart. Only God can regenerate a dead heart and give sight to the blind. This is why apologists should not evaluate their success or adjust their message on the basis of whether the unbeliever finally comes to agree with them or not.[11]

This is one of the truths that alleviates our fear of witnessing. While I want to be as persuasive as I can, it is the Holy Spirit who ultimately convinces the unbeliever of his sin and need of salvation.

Third, the same authority that serves as the basis for our theology (the Scriptures), serves as the basis for our apologetics, too. Even if the unbeliever I am talking to doesn't believe the Bible to be true, I must base my apologetic on the living and powerful Word of God if I want to be as persuasive as possible (Heb. 4:12). We dare not capitulate on that which is the basis for all our arguments. That does not mean that we only quote Scripture in response to arguments against the Christian faith. Rather, in addition to quoting Scripture, we also present our arguments as the consistent outworking of our belief in the Christian worldview as taught in the Bible. After all, if the other person believed the Bible, we couldn't be having an apologetic conversation.

Remember my student from Chapter 2 who asked why I didn't punch my conversation partner in the mouth? He had an argumentative mentality. He thought apologetics was about being contentious and belligerent. Truthfully, not many people are attracted to this kind of engagement, and those who are have the wrong mindset. We want to present sound arguments, but do so in the proper manner.

Conclusion

The power of apologetics is not our own power of persuasion, but rather the power of God the Holy Spirit. While we may have no confidence in our own ability to convince unbelievers of the truth, we should have great confidence in God's ability to use us to persuade others of the truth of the gospel.

Another truth that will give us greater confidence in apologetics is the biblical teaching on the nature of unbelief. By grasping what the Bible says about unbelievers, we can better approach others with the gospel and more effectively answer their objections against the Christian faith.

Chapter Four

Understanding Unbelievers

I groaned inwardly as I sat down next to the businessman on the plane. He was dressed in an expensive suit and was talking loudly on his cell phone about derivatives and futures. I had been hoping to share Christ with someone on the plane but had envisioned someone a little less intimidating.

You see, I grew up in a blue-collar family. My dad was a stone mason, a hard worker who was a little rough around the edges. I didn't understand things like high finance or economics. I related better to people who were more like me. While I knew that this was a divine appointment, I could not overcome the fear of this highly successful captain of industry. Everything about him screamed upper-class—his shoes, his watch, his expensive haircut, and his demanding demeanor. Instead of boldly proclaiming Christ, I turned to my book and guiltily ignored him the entire flight.

What happened? I prejudged him. I looked at his outward appearance and determined that he would not respond positively to a gospel presentation. And in doing so, I committed three errors. First, I acted as if I knew his heart. Only God knows the heart, so I was pretending to be God by imagining

I knew how he would respond. Second, I was committed to only sharing the gospel with people whom I calculated would respond positively. I was not willing to engage someone in a gospel conversation whom I thought would respond with derision or condescension. This revealed my fear of rejection and love for the praise of others.

Finally, I denied something I knew to be true—that this man needed Jesus, no matter whether he thought he needed Him or not. I anticipated that he would tell me that he had all he needed of this world's goods and that he had need of nothing (Rev. 3:17). I didn't know what I would say if he made that claim. I forgot that God has a strong message for those who think they need nothing (Lk. 12:16–21). I forgot that the Scriptures tell us that all people, great and small, share the same condition of estrangement from God and need more than anything to be reconciled to him. I let fear cloud these truths from my mind and keep me from participating in God's call to this man to repent and believe.

Fear!

One of the primary reasons Christians do not share their faith freely is fear. This fear comes in many forms. Some are afraid to be mocked or ridiculed. Others are afraid that they will be asked questions they can't answer. Some fear the high levels of discomfort they experience when they do try to witness. Others fear that they may experience persecution of some kind.

One of the most important truths that can be learned to alleviate fear in witnessing is the nature of unbelievers according to the Bible. In other words, God tells us in his Word exactly what is happening inside the heart and mind of every unbeliever. By learning this, believers can approach unbelievers with more confidence, knowing that regardless of his appearance, every unbeliever shares the same basic characteristics in relation to God.

You Don't Have to Prove God Exists!

Although Scripture has much to say about the nature of unbelievers, no passage is as clear and definitive as Romans 1. This chapter provides a detailed description from God's view of the inner workings of the unregenerate human heart. By coming to understand the Bible's teaching in this chapter, we can begin to shed the irrational fear of sharing the gospel that often grips us.

Every unbeliever already knows God exists and knows some things about him (Rom. 1:18–21). The question that often arises when people consider sharing their faith is, "What if someone demands that I prove God exists before they will believe?" This is a difficult question, but the answer is surprisingly easy—you don't have to. These verses are clear about what the unbeliever already knows. Repeatedly we are told here that unbelievers already know God and are in a relationship of wrath with Him. In verse 19 we see that what the unbeliever is able to know about God is already clear to him, for the very reason that God has shown it to him. If God shows someone something, it is unmistakable. Verse 20 tells us that even God's invisible attributes are clearly understood by the unbeliever every time he looks at the world. This corresponds with Psalm 19:1–2, which tells us that the heavens proclaim God's glory every day. Theologians call this "natural revelation," and Romans 1:20 tells us that this has been true ever since the world was made.

The net effect of this knowledge is that the unbeliever has no excuse for not believing in God. The phrase "without excuse" is a variation of the Greek word *apologia*, from which we get the word "apologetics." In effect, he has no apologetic—no defense against the accusation God will make on the day of judgment, that he knew God but rejected him, nonetheless. In other words, the unbeliever has no way to plead ignorance before God if he does not believe, because he already knows God exists.

He also knows certain truths about God. Verse 20 tells us that the unbeliever knows quite a bit about God, even though his attributes are invisible to the human eye. The reason this is true is that the knowledge of God is implanted in every person who is born. This implanted knowledge of God is part of being made in the image of God. Being God's image begins with inescapably knowing the One we are called to reflect. Specifically, people know God is eternal, all-powerful, and divine. This last item speaks to God's holiness and otherness. God's deity is contrasted to our creatureliness. He is wholly different than we are because he is God and we are not. In addition, he cannot tolerate sin. God's holiness is the root of his wrath against sin, which has been revealed to every unbeliever (v. 18). That is, the unbeliever knows he is guilty before God.

The implications of this are critical. Every unbeliever I talk to, whether he wants to admit it or not, knows God exists and knows he is guilty before God. Even if he denies knowing God, in his heart he knows God and knows that God's wrath is awaiting him if he does not repent. That means that I am talking to someone who is trying to avoid the obvious—God exists, and every person should believe in him.

The question that arises from this, however, is why some unbelievers resort to atheism and deny God if they know him to be true. How can the Bible say that all unbelievers truly know God?

Like Holding a Beach Ball under Water

Romans 1:18 contains the key to understanding how unbelievers can know God, and yet so many deny he exists. Paul says that they "suppress" the truth unrighteously. That is, they actively resist, in a dishonest fashion, the knowledge of God of which they are quite aware. The word "suppress" means to push down or hold back that which is trying to rise to the surface.

Think about the fun that a beach ball can bring. This large, light, inflatable ball can be batted around, used as a kickball, or launched into the wind to see how far it will go. One thing that you cannot do with a beach ball, however, is to play with it under water. The buoyancy of a beach ball means that while you can with great effort momentarily hold it under water, it will quickly rise to the surface.

In the same way, unbelievers daily push down on the knowledge of God that rises in them through both the implanted knowledge of God and the testimony of the created order that they see and experience every day. This knowledge of God is inescapable, as is the guilt for sin. The only way a person can live with such an in-your-face awareness and not be overwhelmed with God's presence is to resist this knowledge.

Suppression happens in a thousand ways. Some people suppress the truth by turning to other religions, redirecting the worship due to God alone to other deities. This is one of the explanations for why there are so many religions in the world. Every one of them is an attempt to worship something other than the one true God, so that the individual does not have to confess his guilt and accept God's terms for salvation. The truth of this is confirmed in the common attempts by all religions to offer a way for the adherents to offer a sacrifice to atone for their sins. By redirecting their worship to other religions, unbelievers mute the voice of God in their hearts and satisfy themselves that they are fine the way they are.

Another way of suppressing the knowledge of God is through filling their lives with distractions. Some people get busy with their jobs, their hobbies, their possessions, and a thousand other time-consuming activities so they won't have time to think about their souls and eternal destiny. By flooding their schedules with constant busyness, they never have to face up to the darkness within that haunts them.

A third way that people suppress the truth is by drugging themselves with substances that dull the pain of guilt. Drugs, alcohol, food, sex, television, internet, sleep, music, and other substances—many of which are good things within the bounds of God's commandments—are misused to satisfy physically what is wrong spiritually. By exchanging relationship with God for substances that reduce the longing of the soul, some people don't have to face up to their estrangement from God.

A fourth way to suppress the knowledge of God is to simply deny that there is any evidence for God and to refuse to look at anything that claims to be evidence. In this case the individual refuses to listen to arguments for God, and discounts anything that is put forth as evidence. This shows the lack of objectivity in an unbeliever because he doesn't *want* God to exist.

For example, Thomas Nagel, professor of law and philosophy at New York University, expresses this candidly when he writes:

> I speak from experience, being strongly subject to this fear myself: I want atheism to be true and am made uneasy by the fact that some of the most intelligent and well-informed people I know are religious

believers. It isn't just that I don't believe in God and, naturally, hope that I'm right in my belief. It's that I hope there is no God! I don't want there to be a God; I don't want the universe to be like that.[12]

Why would a person knowingly reject something solely on the basis that he didn't want it to be true? The answer is that people reject God because they do not want to be accountable to him. They do not want to believe that they have sinned against a God who will someday call them to account and judge them. The truth or falsity of the situation is beside the point. If a person doesn't want something to be true, he can talk himself into believing that it is, in fact, not true.

Suppression, then, is the common experience of unbelievers everywhere. When you talk to someone who doesn't know Christ, you can be sure that in some way, or in many ways, she is holding back the knowledge of God. One of the strategies of apologetics that will be discussed in later chapters is to ask questions that reveal *how* a person is suppressing the truth, so you can get to the heart of her resistance of God. The reason this is important is because suppression has consequences. When a person fights the knowledge of God, there is a price to pay.

The Consequences of Suppression

First, suppression leads to self-deception. Romans 1 tells us that the unbeliever suppresses what is clear and obvious to him. When a person denies reality long enough, he will be unable to tell when he is wrong. The brain's elasticity, combined with the heart's depravity, can make it such that an unbeliever can thoroughly convince himself that he does not know God. This is the most blatant form of self-deception possible. The implanted knowledge of God that is reinforced by the testimony of the created order is so clear that to deny it is to jeopardize one's ability to think clearly. This is exactly what we see described in Ephesians 4:17–19.

The second consequence of suppression is irrationality. That is, a person who deceives himself will begin to think and act against reason. What is ironic is that many unbelievers accuse Christians of being irrational. They are guilty of the very charge they bring against Christianity.

For example, people who deny the existence of God will, in the same breath, speak of nature and the universe as infinite, powerful, creative, intentional, and benevolent. Neil DeGrasse Tyson, the well-known evolutionary astronomer, speaks of the universe "choosing" him to be a scientist. The characteristics attributed to the universe are all actually true of God, yet these intellectuals refuse to acknowledge God. They would rather credit these properties to an impersonal universe.

Likewise, Richard Dawkins, when pressed about the origins of the universe, is forced to admit that he simply doesn't know from where the first elements that began the universe came. His only solution to the problem is that perhaps aliens seeded the universe with the chemical building blocks that began the Big Bang. That answer, however, simply pushes the question back one level. We then must ask from where the aliens came. In both these examples, when the truth of God is denied, the alternate explanations are completely irrational and should not be believed by thinking people.

The third consequence of suppression is that it leads to idolatry. When a person deceives himself long enough, he begins to think irrationally. And when irrationality takes root in the heart, he will do what no clear-headed person would do—he worships false gods. The irrationality is so strong at this point that the ludicrous nature of his actions escapes the unbeliever. Isaiah 44:9–20 describes the irrationality in vivid terms. A man goes into a forest, chops down a tree, and hauls it home. With half a log of wood he makes a fire and cooks his dinner over it. He takes the other half a log to a craftsman who carves it into an idol and overlays it with gold. He then falls down and worships the idol, even though it is nothing more than firewood.

This is the height of self-deception and irrationality. Yet it is no different than what many people in the modern world do, as they worship what they know cannot restore them to God or satisfy the brokenness of their souls. People worship all kinds of objects, values, and abstract ideas, such as power, fame, sexual allure, wealth, importance, and success. To worship means to give yourself over to and to find your significance in. New Testament scholar G. K. Beale defines an idol as "whatever your heart clings to and relies on for ultimate security."[13] Timothy Keller describes an idol as "anything so central and essential to your life that, should you lose it, your life would feel hardly worth living. An idol has such a controlling position in your heart that you can spend most of your passion and energy, your emotional and financial resources, on it without a second thought."[14] And the truth is, everybody worships something.

David Foster Wallace was a rising star in American literature when he suddenly took his own life at the age of forty-six. A few years before his untimely death, Wallace gave a commencement speech at Kenyon University that spoke powerfully to the inescapable urge to worship in humans. An atheist himself, Wallace delivered this statement in the speech:[15]

> Here's something else that's weird but true: in the day-to day trenches of adult life, there is actually no such thing as atheism. There is no such thing as not worshipping. *Everybody worships.* The only choice we get is what to worship. And the compelling reason for maybe choosing some sort of god or spiritual-type thing to worship—be it JC or Allah, be it YHWH or the Wiccan Mother Goddess, or the Four Noble Truths, or some inviolable set of ethical principles— is that pretty much anything else you worship will eat you alive.
>
> **If you worship money and things**, if they are where you tap real meaning in life, then you will never have enough, never feel you have enough. It's the truth.
>
> **Worship your body and beauty and sexual allure** and you will always feel ugly. And when time and age start showing, you will die a million deaths before they finally grieve you.
>
> **Worship power**, and you will end up feeling weak and afraid, and you will need ever more power over others to numb you to your own fear.
>
> **Worship your intellect**, being seen as smart, you will end up feeling stupid, a fraud, always on the verge of being found out.
>
> But the insidious thing about these forms of worship is they're unconscious.

On one level, we all know this stuff already. It's been codified as myths, proverbs, clichés, epigrams, parables; the skeleton of every great story. The whole trick is keeping the truth up front in daily consciousness.

Wallace confirms the teaching of Romans 1, that everybody worships something. And whatever an individual worships that is not God is an idol. So even atheists who often argue that they don't worship anything cannot escape the fact that they inescapably attach their hopes to something in a manner that is clearly worship.

We have looked at how a person becomes an idolater, but another important question is how people continue in idolatry, even when it is so obvious that they are being irrational in their worship. The rest of Romans 1 explains how it is possible.

The Intellectual Exchanges of Idolatry

In order for an unbeliever to continue to deny what is obvious and plain, she must bargain with her heart and mind. Romans 1:23 calls this an exchange. This is a word drawn from Greek marketplace language, where one object is traded for another, presumably of equal value. The irrationality of unbelief, however, means that something of immense value is exchanged for another thing of far lesser value. Three exchanges are mentioned in Romans 1:23–26. In response to each of these bad trades, God levies a judgment against them.

First, unbelievers trade the glory of the immortal God for the tarnished glory of his creation (v. 23). When God first created the world it perfectly reflected his glory. Nothing in creation was cursed by sin or tarnished in any way. It was all "very good" (Gen. 1:31). After Adam and Eve sinned, however, the creation was cursed. Humans became corrupt, animal life became marked by death and brutality, and the natural order was frustrated (Gen. 3:14–19). No longer able to see God's glory uncorrupted, people quickly turned to idolatry, in which common objects were worshiped.

An example helps us understand this. Let's say a soldier goes off to war and brings with him a photo of his wife. He stares at the picture every day because it gives him courage and hope. He may even speak to the picture, so that he feels as if he is talking to her. When he returns home, we would expect him to set aside the picture and focus on his wife, talk to her, and interact with her. If he kept staring at the photo of his wife while she was present, we would question his sanity. The real is present in all its glory. The image is not needed and doesn't compare to the glory of the real person.

Whether we talk about ancient idols (such as gold statues of animals) or modern idols (career, cars, cash, popularity, power, fame), anything we worship other than God is a mere image, something of greatly diminished glory. We were not made to worship created things, but rather the Creator. When we worship anything less than the God in whose image we are made, we diminish our dignity and endanger our humanity, making us liable to becoming inhuman. This is exactly what is described in Romans 1:31, 2 Timothy 3:2–5, and 2 Peter 2:12, where inhuman and animalistic behavior marks the worst of those who worship created things.

Second, unbelievers trade the truth for a lie (v. 25). Even when they know the truth, unbelievers, apart from the work of the Holy Spirit, do not want to accept the truth of God. To accept the existence of the Christian God who is already clearly known is to acknowledge several distasteful truths. First, to accept the existence of God is to accept his authority over his creation. This means that the unbeliever must acknowledge that God is the rightful sovereign, not human beings. It also means that because the unbeliever is accountable to this authoritative God, he must give account of his actions. Thus, second, to accept the existence of God means that the unbeliever is guilty before God. This is something no one naturally wants to admit. As a result, some people simply deny that they have sinned in any way, or that they are guilty before God. As Laurence J. Peter once remarked, "maybe the atheist cannot find God for the same reason a thief cannot find a policeman."[16]

This exchange lies at the heart of those who can accept lies they know to be untrue. When a person rejects the Christian God for another religion, or for nonbelief altogether, he accepts what he knows to be a lie. Sometimes believing a lie is easier psychologically than facing the truth. Often when parents are told that their child has died, they respond by saying, "No, that's not true. It can't be!" They deny what they know to be true as a self-defense mechanism because the truth is too awful to consider.

In the case of unbelief, however, the exchange of the truth for a lie is not rooted in grief, but in rebellion. The unbeliever will accept *anything* other than the Christian God. This is one reason why there are so many religions in the world. Each is a variety of the human heart saying, "I will believe anything but the truth of who God is." The ultimate expression of this foolish rebellion is denying God altogether (Ps. 14:1). However, atheists, agnostics, and skeptics don't escape belief and worship by denying God. They simply worship other, less visible idols—reason, science, wealth, and more. As G. K. Chesterton said, "It's the first effect of not believing in God that you lose your common sense and can't see things as they are."[17] While nonbelievers often regard Christians as irrational, their rejection of what is obviously true makes them the truly irrational ones (1 Cor. 1:18–25).

Third, unbelievers trade what is natural for what is unnatural (v. 26). The last trade builds on the first two. Once a person turns away from truth and glory and worships images and believes lies, he will live in a way that is the antithesis to God's design. The word *antithesis* means the exact opposite. The unbeliever who suppresses truth long enough will believe that beauty is ugliness and ugliness is beauty. He will believe a moral good like trying to prevent the murder of babies in the womb is evil, and that making abortion free and easy to obtain is a moral good. He will also reject the good of sexuality as God designed it and embrace and endorse perversions of God's design.

In this passage, homosexuality is featured as an illustration of the unnatural. Paul is not saying that homosexuality is necessarily the worst sin one could commit, but rather that homosexuality is the most vivid example of unbelievers declaring something to be good which is so obviously contrary to the design of nature. Homosexual acts are attempts to construct a union similar to sex within marriage, but without the benefit of design for such purposes. At the most basic level of human anatomy and DNA is the complementarian design of heterosexual sex in which body parts fit and are capable of reproduction. Homosexuality cannot fulfill God's intention because it goes contrary to his design.

All unbelief results in some form of unnatural behavior. In the Old Testament, God reminds Israel many times that the idols they worshiped were made out of the same stuff as their firewood. To burn one half of a log in the fire and carve the other half into an idol for worship goes against nature, which tells us that trees cannot hear, speak, walk, or do anything else that only God can do (Ps. 115:1–8; Is. 44:9–20).

Unnatural behavior is a hallmark of someone who is severely suppressing the truth, as is rejecting the truth for a lie and preferring images to real glory. Each of these exchanges is clearly a loss for the unbeliever. He moves farther away from relationship with God and from the life God intends. The more the unbeliever makes these exchanges, the further he descends into blindness (Is. 59:1–13; 2 Cor. 4:4).

The Consequences of Suppression

In response to these exchanges, Romans 1 tells us that God, in judgment, "gave them up" to punishment. This phrase (one Greek word) is used three times in Romans, each time in response to one of the exchanges. It is used in the Gospels to describe Pilate handing Jesus over to be scourged, and Judas handing Jesus over in betrayal. It means "to hand over, to give back, or deliver into the hands of." In other words, God's response is to give those who suppress the truth into the hands of their unbelief. The unbeliever is forced to live with the consequences of his rejection of the truth. What are these consequences?

God hands the unbeliever over to impurity and disgrace. (vv. 24, 26, 28). One of the common characteristics of those who suppress the truth is they specifically don't want God limiting their sexuality. As a result, God gives them over to the lusts of their hearts to the extent that they become "unclean" and "without honor." The idea of being unclean or defiled hearkens back to the Old Testament need to become ritually clean before an Israelite could approach God. Until he cleansed himself according to God's directions, the Israelite remained impure and could not approach God. On the other end of the scale was the pagan worshiper who defiled himself with his debased worship of his gods, brutal sacrifices, and gross immorality. The pagans in Canaan were so inhuman that the land "vomited them out" (Lev. 18:28). When God hands a person over to the lusts of his heart, he has to live with the resulting uncleanness.

God allows unbelievers to dishonor their bodies among themselves and become slaves to their passions. This speaks of the lack of dignity that comes from rejecting God's ways. By rejecting the glory of God, the unbeliever becomes undignified as he who is made in God's image worships animals, birds, and animals that creep along the ground (v. 23). Their minds dwell on the most worthless and beastly thoughts. The list that concludes Romans 1 details the extent of the baseness with twenty-one descriptions of the wickedness of those who suppress the truth. Paul concludes with a stunning statement: Not only do those who do such things know they are deserving of death; they encourage others to do them, too.

Conclusion

This extensive description of unbelievers is a stunning contrast to the way unbelievers, and often Christians, view non-Christians. Things are far worse for the unbeliever than he ever imagines. Yet, this makes the good news all the more glorious. The more a person accepts God's assessment of his heart and estrangement from God, the closer he comes to repentance and faith in Christ. To soften the blow of this description is to blunt the call to repentance, making salvation more difficult to obtain. Only with the conviction of his rebellion and idolatry will the unbeliever be able to see the beauty and rationality of the gospel.

Chapter Five

Destroying Strongholds

"It happened exactly as you said it would!"

One of my apologetics students returned to school in the fall semester, excited about the opportunity he had to share the gospel over the summer. The method we covered in class the previous spring prepared him well for real conversations with unbelievers.

"I was working with a guy and he asked why I was a Christian. I explained that I had come to believe that Jesus was the Son of God who died for my sins and rose again to give me eternal life. He said he didn't believe the Bible was true, and I asked what made him think that."

His coworker, Chris, responded, "Because it's full of errors and has been corrupted through the years."

Brent wasn't fazed and retorted, "Can you give me an example of the errors you say are in the Bible?"

"Well, I don't know. That's just what I heard."

Brent asked another question, "So you can't name any errors, yet the Bible is supposedly full of them. Have you ever read the Bible?"

"Well, no. But how can we even know what it originally said anyway? There's no way it could have lasted this long without major changes to the message."

Brent smiled and said, "Well, how much do the manuscripts of the Bible differ?"

"I don't know. I'm not a historian or Bible scholar," Chris replied.

"Actually, there are thousands of early manuscripts and they agree on more than 95 percent of the words; and where copyists made mistakes, it is relatively easy to spot them. So the Bible is very reliable. In fact, it is arguably the most reliable ancient document we have."

Chris was surprised. "I didn't know that. I was taught in college that the original words were lost and that no one really knows what it said."

Brent continued, "So what do you believe about God and the meaning of life?"

"I suppose I am agnostic. I don't know if God exists or if we can even know if he does."

"What has led you to believe that?"

As the conversation continued, Brent kept asking questions that challenged Chris' beliefs, and each time he did Chris found himself unable to support his views. In the end Brent was able to present the gospel to a more open Chris, who was wondering what happened to the ideas he held so strongly one hour before.

Challenging the Authority of the Unbeliever's Worldview

In the previous chapter we gained a clear view of the hearts and minds of unbelievers; now we are prepared to talk about engaging them with the gospel. In this chapter we will explore the indirect method of apologetics that flows naturally from a presuppositional approach. This indirect method teaches Christians to ask the right kind of questions that undermine the unbelieving worldview of the non-Christian. The benefit of this approach is that it takes pressure off the Christian to have all the answers. It places the burden on the unbeliever to justify his objection to the Christian faith. This approach is relatively easy to learn, and so is accessible to the average Christian.

In 2 Corinthians 10:3–5, Paul explains that the battles that we fight are not physical, but spiritual battles. As a result, the weapons we use are not swords or guns, but rather truth and ideas. In the ancient world, cities were surrounded by high, thick walls. The walls were the first line of defense. Inside the walls, however, was a stronghold where the city stored supplies to outlast a siege. The stronghold was also a place to which the city leaders could retreat if the walls were breached until help would arrive. If the stronghold was brought down or breached, all was lost and those inside had to surrender to survive.

This is the word picture Paul uses to describe the tactic Christians should use when interacting with unbelievers. We should try to discern the authority (stronghold) on which the unbeliever relies. For some people, the authority is human reason; for others, science is their authority. Other authorities on which people rely include religion, a particular thinker, parents, or their own experience. On whatever authority the unbeliever bases his ideas and values, that is the stronghold in his life.

Once the stronghold is identified we can begin to challenge that authority. By undermining the authority in which the unbeliever trusts, we take away from him the grounds of his objections to the gospel. This approach echoes the wisdom saying in Proverbs 21:22: "A wise man scales the city of the mighty and brings down the stronghold in which they trust." Even though an intellectual stronghold can be difficult to bring down, Paul reminds us that Christians have been given divine power to do so. This is no magical power, but one found in the arguments themselves. As he says in verse 5 of the above passage, we "destroy arguments." That is, the arguments we use to defeat the objections raised against the Christian faith are powerful by virtue of being true. Truth is always more powerful than falsehood.

In our conversations with unbelievers, we are seeking to show the weakness and incoherence of the unbeliever's worldview. We do this with the confidence that even though we can't always see weakness in his arguments at first, they are there. Only the Christian faith can coherently answer the deep questions of meaning in life. The more we interact with unbelievers and seek to identify their strongholds, the better we become at identifying them accurately. When we identify them accurately, we can show how the stronghold cannot stand the scrutiny of truth. But how do we do this?

The Role of Questions

The key to engaging unbelievers in a nonthreatening way is to *ask questions*. This approach has several advantages. First, asking questions encourages the conversation to continue. This is a basic principle of human relationships—people like to talk about themselves. By asking questions about the other person, conversation is encouraged.

It is easy to see that this approach to evangelism is different than others that are often practiced. Some people who evangelize focus their efforts primarily on distributing literature such as tracts. This approach often aims for quantity—give out as many tracts as possible, with as minimal interaction as possible with those who take them. While tracts can be helpful as a summary of the gospel to be read at a later time, those who use them sometimes do so to avoid real conversations with unbelievers.

Another approach to evangelism is what one author calls "the gospel burp." This amounts to a monologue with the unbeliever, in which the Christian tries to blurt out as much of the gospel as possible before the unbeliever cuts him off. This is called the gospel burp because the gospel is blurted out as fast as possible, the Christian feels good afterward, and the unbeliever feels assaulted.

The approach we are advocating here, however, is a genuine engagement in conversation with the unbeliever. It starts by showing interest in the person and asking questions that get to the heart of the unbeliever's worldview and belief system. After beginning a conversation, the Christian may steer the conversation toward spiritual matters any number of ways. An effective segue may be something like, "So, what is your religious background?" Or equally effective would be something like, "So, what do you value most in life?" The key here is to move the conversation as naturally as you can into questions of ultimate meaning. Cornelius Van Til described this as carrying the Bible in one hand and a newspaper in the other. In other words, almost anything—including current events, cultural events (such as music, film, literature, etc.), or common interests—can be used to transition to spiritual matters.

I have frequently started conversations with people by asking about the book they are reading, the meaning of the tattoo on their arm, the message of their t-shirt, or a sticker on their laptop. These natural conversation starters flow easily into discussions of meaning and values. Around the time I began learning about apologetics, the book *The DaVinci Code* became popular. I was flying back from a teaching trip to Ukraine and sat next to a woman on the plane who was reading it. I had not heard of the book, so I asked her about it. She gushed about the book and its view that the New Testament had been corrupted by those who wanted to remove the feminine and the goddess element in early Christianity. By asking about the book, our conversation naturally flowed into questions of the reliability of the Bible and the person of Christ.

Once the conversation turns toward spiritual matters, the questions continue. If an unbeliever has a religious background, you can then ask something like, "Tell me about how that affected your beliefs," or "I don't know much about that religion/denomination. Tell me more about it." This is a genuine request, as you should be interested in discovering as much as you can about the person, so that when you begin to share the gospel, you know how to target your presentation to the non-Christian's actual beliefs. If the unbeliever has no religious background or has rejected belief in God, you can ask a question such as, "Why don't you believe in God?" or "What made you lose your faith?"

The key here is to *listen*. To avoid the offense of the gospel burp, we must take the time to listen to unbelievers explain why they don't believe. We must listen to the stories of how they lost their faith, or never had any. Remember, evangelism and apologetics should flow out of a genuine interest in and love for that person. Listening and asking follow-up questions demonstrates respect and gentleness, and often opens the door for you to challenge her unbelief and present the gospel.

Once the non-Christian begins to tell about what she believes, you can begin to ask questions that push below the surface, to the *reason* why she believes what she does. These are seemingly safe questions that force her to justify her own belief system. Some common questions include:

- Why do you believe that?
- What do you base that on?
- Where did you get that idea?
- What makes you think that?
- How do you know that?
- What do you mean by that?
- Can you give me an example of that?
- What led you to believe that?

These are all variations on a theme, and they make her think about the grounds for believing what she believes. The truth is, many people have not thought too deeply about *why* they believe what they believe. The answers to these questions will begin to reveal the authorities in which she trusts. For example, what if she says, "I believe we all just evolved, and that fate rules the universe"? That kind of statement is nearly impossible to answer directly, because it is so vague and involves such complicated ideas as evolution and fate. Rather than answering or arguing against this statement, ask one of the questions above.

Asking questions is the key to making progress with unbelievers. This has several advantages over a full-frontal assault on ideas opposing the Christian faith. First, as mentioned previously, asking questions encourages the conversation to continue, as opposed to expressing disagreement bluntly. In our increasingly secular society, people are easily put off by disagreement. Although sometimes we have to disagree bluntly, if we can demonstrate the irrationality and contradiction of unbelief, the non-Christian is more likely to forfeit false beliefs. Second, asking questions prevents the Christian from having to possess extensive knowledge of philosophy, science, history, and other academic fields. The truth is, the average Christian will never become conversant in these areas. Asking questions, however, removes the burden of having to know so much. The non-Christian shares the details of her beliefs so the Christian knows exactly what error he is trying to refute. It allows the Christian to place the burden of knowledge on the unbeliever who is rejecting Christianity, and it can also expose if she is merely bluffing and does not have ground on which to stand.

The third advantage of asking questions is that it allows the unbeliever to arrive at conclusions about his worldview and belief system on his own without you telling him he is wrong. The goal is to ask the right kind of questions, so that he comes to see for himself that his beliefs are a problem. Self-discovery is powerful when it comes to belief systems. This is what is known as the *subversive power* of the gospel. To subvert something means to undermine it and overthrow it. The gospel destabilizes, disrupts, and sabotages belief systems constructed out of suppression of the truth. The key to doing this well and bringing the unbeliever closer to Christ is to ask good questions.

Christian thinker Os Guinness, explains this well:

> Questions are always more subversive than statements. For one thing, they are indirect. Whereas it should be crystal clear what a statement is saying and where it is leading, a good question is not so obvious,

and where it leads to is hidden. For another thing, questions are involving. Whereas a statement always has a "take it or leave it" quality, and we may or may not be interested in what it tells us, there is no standing back from a well-asked question. It invites us, challenges us or intrigues us to get into it and follow it to see where it leads. In short, even a simple question can be a soft form of subversion.[18]

As mentioned earlier, questions invite further conversation. This makes the encounter with the unbeliever more natural and less strained. The unbeliever does not feel like she has encountered a salesman, but a satisfied customer (to put it crassly). Instead of being awkward, the conversation feels more like a person who has been healed of a deadly disease telling another sick person where to find healing.

Imagine the unbeliever's worldview as a wall of bricks that she has constructed around herself to keep the truth from pressing in on her heart and mind. Every brick in the wall is a different belief, experience, and opinion that she has built up to make herself feel justified in rejecting the truth. By asking questions and showing that her beliefs are contradictory or irrational, you are removing these bricks one by one. The more you can cause her to doubt her own beliefs, the less protection she has in her unbelief and the fewer reasons she has to keep rejecting the truth. Therefore, no matter how far the conversation goes, as long as some bricks are dislodged or removed, the encounter is a victory.

I often need this reminder when my encounter with an unbeliever does not seem to go far. My hope in a shortened conversation is to challenge or undermine confidence in at least one belief. My God-ordained role in any encounter may be nothing more than loosening one brick. I hope it is greater than that, but if I can even loosen or dislodge one brick of unbelief, I can see the encounter as a success.

Effective Interaction Using Questions and Challenges

Asking questions and providing answers is not always a straightforward venture. There are several keys to making progress in your encounters with the unbeliever.

First, ask clarifying questions. As you ask questions and the unbeliever explains what he believes, ask questions from time to time to make sure you understand his position. If he says something unclear, such as that he couldn't believe in such a complex God as Christianity presents, ask, "What do you mean by 'complex' in this situation?" Sometimes people make vague or confusing arguments that are not clear at all. Be sure to ask for clarification so you don't talk past one another. This is especially important in conversations with members of cults, because they will often use the same language as a Christian. You may also ask him to define his terms, because if you both have a different understanding of an issue or concept, you will not be able to effectively communicate. Other clarifying questions include, "Am I understanding you correctly?", "Are you saying that . . .?", and "Is it fair to say that you are arguing [X position]?"

One time I was sitting next to an engineer and as our conversation turned to Christianity, he objected on the grounds that it was not rational to believe in God. No matter what I said, his response centered on the irrationality of believing what we couldn't prove scientifically. Finally, I realized that he was trying to determine the concept of what was rational and what was irrational. I asked him, "You keep using the term 'rational.' What is rationality, and who gets to define it?" He stopped as he realized that since rationality is not an object in the physical world to be studied, he had to justify what he meant by "rational." That required more than he was prepared to admit. Our discussion turned away from whether Christianity was rational to what was rationality. He was honest enough to admit that this was a harder question and that he could not prove his definition was better or even correct.

Second, restate the position. Once you understand what the non-Christian believes, restate his position in simple terms. This is an important step, because once he affirms that you properly understand him, you can move on to the next step. For example, if he says that he believes that evolution explains everything in the universe, clarify by saying something like, "So you are saying that everything comes about randomly through time and chance?" This helps him see that if he wants to hold to Darwin's theory of evolution, there are intellectual consequences. This is an important step, because once he affirms that you properly understand him, you can move on to the next step.

Third, take his position for the sake of argument. Once you understand what the non-Christian believes, the next step is to take his position for the sake of argument and show him the implications. For example, he may argue that everything came about randomly by time and chance, but that we should still do good to people and not harm. Show him that if everything came about randomly by time and chance, we can't say that anything is necessarily right or wrong. Anything that develops randomly is just that—random. Whatever happens in the universe just *is*. He has no grounds to say it is good or bad. A sense of right or wrong that everyone ought to obey cannot come from a universe that is random. In forcing him to hold his position consistently with all its implications, you are demonstrating that his beliefs are irrational or a contradiction.

By taking his position and holding it consistently, you are showing him that beliefs should be coherent; they should relate to one another. Some beliefs are the basis of other beliefs. Other beliefs are the necessary consequences of those basic beliefs. For example, if someone is a *nihilist* (someone who believes that life has no meaning), then logical consequences of that belief include that there is nothing worth living for, no action is better than another, and suicide makes sense. If he is a nihilist, yet wants to use his life in service of humanity, you want to point out that doing so is no better than living only for yourself, because he has already started with the idea that life has no meaning.

This step is often a moment of awakening for unbelievers, as they realize that their beliefs contradict each other. By asking good questions and playing along with their worldview with all its implications, you help them see for themselves the error of their thinking.

Fourth, call his bluff. Sometimes in his opposition to the Christian faith the unbeliever will spout "facts" and "statistics" that seem to strengthen his case for unbelief. Often these arguments will pertain to topics you may not be familiar with. This can make you feel like you have lost the case for Christianity, because you don't know how to answer him. The truth is, however, that many times the unbeliever is bluffing. He may be making up his information or may be quoting someone else in error. This happens more often than you might think.

For example, someone who has heard a skeptic on the radio or read an Internet article that attacks Christianity will often use those "facts" in a discussion with a Christian. Many times, however, he will get the facts wrong, misquote the source, or even misunderstand the source altogether. When unbelievers challenge the reliability of Scripture or some cultural element in the biblical story that seems foreign to us in the twenty-first century, they often raise objections about things of which they know little. The truth is that the average Christian knows more about the ancient Near Eastern world of the Old Testament and the first-century world of the New Testament than the average unbeliever, simply from hearing sound, biblical preaching in church. So when the unbeliever tries to attack some aspect of the Bible or the Christian faith, he often has no idea what he is talking about.

In these cases, the Christian should "call the bluff" of the unbeliever. In other words, if you hear a "fact" that supposedly proves Christianity wrong, or challenges the truth, question it. Going back to our questions above, ask, "Where did you hear that?" or "What is your source for that fact?" or "Can you prove that statistic reliably?" Often you will find that the unbeliever has no idea where his argument came from and no way to substantiate his claim. By calling his bluff you are pulling him back to real facts. And the Christian faith deals in real, historically verified facts (1 Cor. 15:1–20).

When an objection to the Christian faith *is* based in historical fact, we don't have to worry that it somehow proves Christianity wrong. Historical facts have to be interpreted, and while some critics may interpret a fact to be destructive to the truth claim of Christianity, there are always other scholars who interpret the fact to be supportive of the truth of the faith. For example, some critics would say that the fact that the disciples were not expecting the resurrection of Jesus proves that Jesus never taught that he would rise again, and that the resurrection never truly happened.

Many other scholars however counter that claim by showing that since the disciples did not expect the resurrection, the story could not have been made up by them. People trying to pass off a lie as the truth do not fabricate details that are unbelievable. The fact that the Gospel accounts report the resurrection speaks strongly to its authenticity.

By learning these four tactics of asking questions and challenging the unbeliever's objections, a Christian can make great progress in disarming the unbeliever's opposition to Christianity. What comes next is a more direct response to the objections raised.

Destroy Arguments and Pull Down Strongholds

As you ask questions and challenge the unbeliever's worldview indirectly, you will now begin to weave into the conversation more direct confrontation of her beliefs. By this time, you have already debunked some of her cherished beliefs, and if the conversation continues, she will be more open to hearing alternative explanations of the issues for which she no longer has answers. There are several ways to begin to present the Christian faith more directly.

First, challenge her errors and misconceptions about Christianity. While you are interacting with the unbeliever, pay attention to any "facts" she proposes about Christianity. Many times, unbelievers will make accusations about the Bible or the Christian faith that are simply wrong. In such a case, you must correct that error before proceeding with the conversation.

For example, if the unbeliever says, "I just can't believe in a God who toys with people's lives and punishes them for no reason whatsoever." If you are not listening carefully, you might try to defend this view of God, when in fact Christians don't believe in this portrayal of God. This description is a distortion of the biblical concepts of God's sovereignty and justice. A proper response would be something like, "Oh, I don't believe in that type of God either. Can I tell you about the God I *do* believe in?" In other words, don't let misconceptions about the Christian faith stand without correction.

Similarly, if someone says, "I believe in Jesus! I believe he was a wise teacher who taught people to love one another and be at peace. I just don't believe that Jesus would ever condemn people or only make one way to God," a good response would be, "Jesus was a wise teacher and he did teach us to love one another, but he also spoke of judgment. He did claim to be the only way to God. If you are going to be fair with the evidence and not make up a Jesus of your own liking, then you have to consider everything he did and said, not just the parts you like." By doing this you are making sure that the unbeliever understands the Christian faith accurately.

On a flight a few years ago, I sat next to one of the friendliest and outgoing people I have ever met. Our conversation began as soon as we settled into our seats and continued the entire two-hour flight. Stefan was funny and cheerful, the kind of person you hope to sit next to when flying (if you are an extrovert like me). As the conversation turned toward the gospel, he affirmed his respect for Jesus and expressed his admiration for his virtuous life, except for that one time Jesus sinned. I did a double take and asked him what he meant when he said that Jesus sinned.

"You know, that one time where the Bible said that Jesus sinned," Stefan repeated.

I replied, "I'm not sure what you are talking about, because the Bible never says that Jesus sinned."

He was genuinely surprised. "Come on," he continued, "you know that time when Jesus' mother asked him to turn water into wine and he snapped at her."

I explained that Jesus' response was neither snappy nor a sin.

"Wow, all this time I thought Jesus had sinned, so I never thought of him as the perfect Son of God."

Having cleared up his misunderstanding, I proceeded to share with him what the Gospels tell us about Jesus' teachings and life. Had that not come up in conversation, Stefan would have continued to believe Jesus was just a good man.

Second, contrast the irrationality and contradiction of unbelief with the wisdom and rationality of the Christian faith. As you help the unbeliever realize that his worldview is inconsistent, irrational, and contradictory by asking questions, you also want to interject the aspects of the Christian faith that provide real answers to those very questions. This is the aspect of apologetics that seeks to commend the Christian faith for its beauty and wisdom. I want to help the unbeliever see that the Christian faith meets all the intellectual tests that it encounters. The Christian faith can answer every legitimate challenge raised against it.

But there's more. The gospel of Jesus Christ answers the deepest longings of the human heart. The reason this is so is because Christianity is about a relationship with a person—the God-man, Jesus Christ. What the unbeliever really wants in his soul, as one who was made to be in relationship with God, is to be restored to him. Therefore, you want to present the gospel clearly and in a compelling fashion. The truth should be attractive. Even as you are removing the bricks in the wall of his worldview, you are presenting the alternative of Christ as the real answer to his longings.

This step is crucial; otherwise you may seem like nothing more than someone who likes to deconstruct the views of others. If you can present the logic and beauty of the Christian faith, you show the unbeliever that there is somewhere to go once he has rejected his former views. In order to do this, the Christian needs to know his faith as thoroughly as possible. The more you understand all that the Christian faith teaches, the more thoroughly you will be able to describe the merits of the Christian faith. Second Corinthians 4:6 tells us that everything humans seek—knowledge, light, and glory—are all found in knowing Christ.

Third, if you don't know the answer to a question or objection, say so. Just as we should call the bluff of unbelievers who try to present phony evidence and unsubstantiated arguments against Christianity, we ourselves should always avoid bluffing. Unbelievers are keen to sense when a Christian is making up evidence or arguments for the faith. One of the most powerful things you can do when encountering a question or challenge to which you don't know the answer is to say those three little words: "I don't know."

Many people think that doing this is to admit defeat, but in reality, not knowing the answer to an unbeliever's question shows that you are a real person. No one can know the answer to every question or objection that may be raised against the Christian faith. The truth is, there are a thousand objections about minor points of Christian doctrine or the Bible that can be raised, many of them obscure and inconsequential. An unbeliever may spend much time learning one of these objections, while ignoring the weight of Christian evidence. All but the best Christian scholars would find it difficult to be prepared for every possible objection, so don't put that pressure on yourself. If you don't know how to answer an objection, just say so. Doing this will give you credibility as a humble, genuine person who doesn't try to bluff his way through a defense of the faith.

As a follow-up to admitting you don't have an answer you can say, "I don't know, but I will find an answer and get back to you. Can we plan to meet soon so you can hear my answer?" An honest unbeliever won't expect you to know the answer to every question and will usually respect a sincere admission.

Conclusion

This chapter contains a significant amount of instruction and advice regarding the proper method of apologetics. Learning to incorporate this method of engaging unbelievers takes considerable practice. The best way to learn, however, is not to keep reading and studying until you feel super-confident, with no doubts left regarding your ability. That day will simply never come. No, the way to grow in your ability is to remind yourself of these truths, and then to just go do it. Engage non-Christians in conversation. Start by asking questions about their worldview and then begin to incorporate these ideas little by little. No amount of study will replace actual encounters with unbelievers. By doing apologetics to the best of your ability, you will build up your skill in answering questions and pointing people to the gospel of Christ.

One thing that is especially important to remember is that conversion is a work of the Holy Spirit. God is the one who saves; you are merely the messenger of the truth. Be sensitive to how much the unbeliever can take at one time. If she shows interest in the Christian faith, keep going! If after a while she seems to want to stop the conversation, model the gentleness and respect commanded in 1 Peter 3:16, and end the conversation graciously. Trust that the Holy Spirit will continue to use your words to convict and draw the unbeliever long after you are done speaking with her.

This chapter shows that anyone can do apologetics. Anyone can learn to ask good questions. Anyone can learn to share the truth of the gospel in a clear and compelling fashion. May your efforts in this venture yield abundant fruit in the lives of the unbelievers that God brings across your path!

Chapter Six

Getting Them to Jesus

What is the gospel? Is it only about what happens to a person at death, or does it have implications now? Is salvation a lifelong process or a one-time event (or something else)? Is it about a person's relationship with God, or is it liberation from oppressive social and economic structures? Is it the same as an invitation to church or a challenge to be moral? Unless we are clear about where we are trying to lead our unbelieving conversation partner, we may find ourselves defending a general belief in God instead of the heart of Christianity itself. We may successfully defend the faith, but not know how to bring the conversation around to an invitation to anything in particular.

We have come this far in the book and have not even addressed this question in any depth. Yet the end goal of apologetics is evangelism—leading another person to repent and place her trust in Jesus Christ for salvation. At the same time you are challenging the unbeliever's worldview, you want to begin sharing the good news of Jesus. Many Christians are not aware of the powerful claims Jesus made while on earth. Many are also unaware that compared to every other religion and belief system, only the Christian faith has the ability to explain the human condition and answer the deepest questions of the human heart. This chapter focuses on some of Christianity's strongest arguments and equips students to know the strength of the claims for the truth of Christianity.

Planting and Watering

One of the reasons we hesitate to begin a gospel conversation with unbelievers is that we don't know where to go with it. Even if we do know how to lead someone to Christ, we may hesitate if we don't think that person would become a Christian on the spot. Some people feel that if sharing the gospel doesn't result in conversion right then and there, the whole effort is a failure.

One liberating truth of evangelism and apologetics is that God has not called us to convert people to the gospel, but simply to share, in a persuasive fashion, the good news of the gospel. *Any* progress that is made in sharing the truth of the gospel is a success. If the Holy Spirit is the one who convinces and convicts, then any progress made in talking about the unbeliever's worldview and beliefs, or about Jesus and the Christian faith, is a successful encounter.

The apostle Paul used the image of planting and watering seeds when he spoke of the contributions that he and Apollos made in proclaiming the gospel and planting churches (1 Cor. 3:5–9). He acknowledges that *we* are not the difference-makers in someone's salvation—*God* is. We do, however, have an important part to play in the process of someone coming to faith in Christ. God often works through secondary means to accomplish his work. When a Christian proclaims the gospel, destroys intellectual strongholds, or challenges unbelief, he is planting and watering seeds in the heart and mind of unbelievers.

This truth should relieve the pressure from us when we think about engaging unbelievers in conversation. God the Holy Spirit is the one doing the great work of reaching the unbeliever, not us. We are those who simply speak the truth to the degree that God opens the door for conversation. We can, without pressure or anxiety, communicate as much of the truth as possible, and leave the result with God. For many people, this simple reality removes the element of fear, because they know they can trust God to do his part. The Christian can walk away from every encounter rejoicing that no matter how far the conversation progressed, it was a divine success.

Get Them to Jesus

What is the goal of evangelism and apologetics? It is not to argue endlessly, or to merely agree to disagree. The goal is very simple: Get them to Jesus. In other words, the goal is to dismantle the unbeliever's worldview so effectively, and present Jesus so compellingly, that her heart is led to repentance and faith in Christ. This truth should guide everything we do when in conversation with non-Christians. This is the very essence of the gospel.

In our apologetic efforts we are not seeking merely to convince unbelievers that God exists, or that the historical Jesus exists. We are not proclaiming a message of moral transformation or social good. The gospel message is clear—guilty sinners can find reconciliation with God through the person and work of Jesus Christ. A clear gospel presentation requires us to address the unbeliever's guilt before God because of her sin, and her need to repent. The good news of the gospel is that God has provided a sacrifice for sins through the life, death, and resurrection of Christ; and that salvation is obtained by faith in Jesus, apart from a person's own merit. Saving faith in Jesus brings forgiveness of sin, reconciliation to God, eternal life, the indwelling of the Holy Spirit, and union with Jesus Christ.

We must keep this end in mind the entire time we engage unbelievers. If we don't, we may stop with simply answering objections. We are hoping for nothing less than a transition from wrath to grace for the unbeliever in his relationship to God. This goal, however, seems so far away when we encounter people who reject the Christian faith on multiple grounds. How do we move a person from rejection to acceptance of the gospel message?

The answer is to focus on Jesus.

As you ask and answer questions, clear away intellectual obstacles, and present the Christian alternative, the primary goal is to get him to consider the claims and work of Christ on the cross. This only makes sense. If what saves a person is trust in who Jesus is and what he said and did in his incarnation, then you want to try to talk about those topics as soon as the unbeliever is ready to listen and consider them. As soon as some of his objections are answered, you want to begin to introduce the gospel truths about Jesus—his divinity, his incarnation, his humanity, his life and death, and his resurrection. What a person does with Jesus determines his eternal state, so nothing else is as important.

This is the primary reason we don't get involved in arguments about issues that don't really matter. Paul warned Timothy to rebuke those in the church who spent time in pointless questions and speculations about matters of minor importance compared to the gospel (1 Tim. 1:3–7). It is too easy to get off track in discussions with unbelievers about the age of the earth, the details of the end times, or a person's views on cultural issues. While these may be important in other contexts, they have nothing to do with a person's salvation. You want to focus on the central claims of Jesus to be God in the flesh, the only way to restoration with God, and the risen Savior.

Therefore, when engaging with unbelievers, focus on clearing away objections so that they can hear and consider the claims of Jesus in Scripture. What are the key claims of the Bible about Jesus and by Jesus of which people are often unaware?

The Historical Nature of the Christian Gospel

First, Jesus was a verifiable historical figure. Some claim that Jesus never existed, that he was a legend, or that he was a compilation of first-century sages and revolutionaries. In other words, this objection argues that either we cannot really know whether Jesus existed due to the unreliable nature of the documents that describe him—or more stridently, that no reliable evidence exists whatsoever, and therefore there is no reason to believe he actually lived.

This objection is common among those who don't want to argue the question of Jesus at all. If they can dismiss his existence, then nothing the Bible says about him really matters. The problem, however, is that historians, both Christian and non-Christian, are almost universally agreed that Jesus existed. In his book *Did Jesus Exist?*, atheist New Testament scholar Bart Ehrman provides a detailed response to those who want to deny the historical reality of Jesus.[19] A premiere historian himself, Ehrman argues that any true historian has to admit that Jesus existed, and that there are certain aspects of the Jesus story that are indisputable. He argues this point on the basis of what historians look for when they try to establish a historical fact based on the evidence. Even though Ehrman doesn't accept many of the details of Jesus' life and teaching to be true, he would argue that to dismiss the historical evidence of Jesus is to call the very study of history into question.

What establishes historical facts? First, eyewitness accounts that exhibit carefulness in the reporting of facts shows that the testimony was not merely a legend or fable. The Gospels provide multiple eyewitness accounts, along with carefully researched accounts of Jesus' life, ministry, and death (Jn. 1:14; 1 Jn. 1:1–3; Lk. 1:1–4). Second, events taking place in public view in a historically verified location where falsehoods could be exposed puts the historical event under scrutiny. Unlike the sacred writings of many other religions, the New Testament mentions hundreds of historically verifiable names, dates, places, events, towns, geographical features, and more.

Third, confirming evidence from a hostile source lends credence to the event, because if a disbeliever of the meaning of an event agrees that it happened, there is high likelihood of its historical reliability. For example, the Jewish authorities who opposed Jesus admitted that the tomb was empty on the third day, both in the Bible (Matt. 28:11–15), and nonbiblical sources (the Toledath Jesu, a compilation of early Jewish writings).

Fourth, well-known people are included in the gospel stories, and had the accounts been fictitious, they could have been easily refuted. For example, in the burial account after Jesus' crucifixion, Joseph of Arimathea is mentioned as the one who buries Jesus in his own tomb. Joseph was too well-known for a legend to arise about him without it being exposed as false.

Many other criteria of history could be mentioned, but it is clear that the historical evidence for Jesus is solidly on the side of what Christians believe about him.

Jesus Claimed to Be God

Jesus claimed to be God. Many people have never considered what a radical claim this is. Jesus claimed to be God in human form. This means that Jesus could not have been simply a good teacher or a wise, wandering sage, as many people believe. C. S. Lewis addresses this dilemma in his famous "trilemma" discussion:

> I am trying here to prevent anyone saying the really foolish thing that people often say about Him: "I'm ready to accept Jesus as a great moral teacher, but I don't accept His claim to be God." That is the one thing we must not say. A man who said the sort of things Jesus said would not be a great moral teacher. He would either be a lunatic—on a level with the man who says he is a poached egg—or else he would be the Devil of Hell. You must make your choice. Either this man was, and is, the Son of God: or else a madman or something worse. You can shut Him up for a fool, you can spit at Him and kill Him as a demon; or you can fall at His feet and call Him Lord and God. But let us not come with any patronizing nonsense about His being a great human teacher. He has not left that open to us. He did not intend to.[20]

In other words, what people often believe about Jesus, that he was merely a good, moral teacher, cannot be true because of the claims he made to be God in the flesh. A good, moral person does not claim to be God. But Jesus did, in fact, claim to be God.

Sometimes critics argue this point by pointing out that Jesus never said the particular phrase, "I am God." This is a false test of the deity of Christ, however, because the truth of a statement does not depend on particular wording if there are other ways to describe the truth. I don't have to say, "I am a father" to establish that truth. I can talk about my children, and in doing so I state indirectly the obvious—that I am a father. In the same way, there are many different ways Jesus makes it clear that he is claiming to be God. In addition, the reactions of others when he used these various ways to state his deity demonstrate that those who heard him understood him to be claiming to be God.

In John 3:13–15 Jesus claims to have come from heaven and to be the Son of Man. The term "Son of Man" does not speak primarily of Jesus' humanity, but rather his deity. It is an allusion to Daniel 7:13–14 where the Son of Man is equated with God himself. This term is used more than eighty times in the New Testament, many of them by Jesus referring to himself.

In John 5:18–26 the Jewish leaders wanted to kill Jesus because he was making himself equal to God. How was he doing that? He was comparing his miraculous works with God's work (v. 17). This alone, in the minds of the Jews, was a claim to be God.

In John 8:58 Jesus used the words of God in the Old Testament to describe himself. As God told Moses, "I AM who I AM," Jesus claimed the same status for himself by saying that, "Before Abraham was, I AM." The very next verse shows that the Jews interpreted this as another claim to deity, because they picked up rocks in order to stone him for his blasphemy. Jesus did not seek to correct them for their interpretation of his words, thus leaving his claim intact.

In John 10:30–33 Jesus says, "I and the Father are one." Again, the Jews picked up rocks to stone Jesus. He asked them why they wanted to kill him, and their response showed that they interpreted his words as a claim to deity. Additional claims to deity can be found in the following passages: Mark 14:61–62; Mark 2:1–12; Matthew 26:63–65; Luke 22:67–70; John 16:28.

Jesus Claimed to Be the Messiah

Jesus claimed to be the Messiah who had been promised in the Old Testament. This is an especially helpful claim if the person to whom you are talking is Jewish, but it also refutes objections about the God of the Old Testament being different from the God of the New Testament, or the objection that Christianity evolved from Old Testament religion. If Jesus fulfilled what the Old Testament promised, then there is no conflict between the Old and New Testaments.

In John 5:39 and 46, Jesus claimed that all the Old Testament Scripture spoke of him. In Luke 24:27 Jesus showed the two disciples on the road to Emmaus that the whole Old Testament pointed forward to his life, death, and resurrection. In Matthew 5:17–18 Jesus told the crowds gathered to hear him on the mountain that he came to fulfill the law, not do away with it. In addition, Jesus fulfilled more than three hundred specific prophecies in the Old Testament.

Jesus Claimed to Be the Only Way to Be Reconciled to God

In John 14:6 Jesus explicitly claims to be the only way to God, the ultimate truth, and the only source of life. Showing an unbeliever that Jesus claimed to be the exclusive way to be reconciled to God refutes the idea that Jesus only thought of himself as one possible way to God. If there are many ways to God, and Jesus claimed to be the only way, this would make Jesus egotistical, narrowminded, and bigoted. Therefore, he could not be just a good, moral teacher. He either is the only way to God, or he isn't and is not worthy to be followed.

Jesus Rose from the Dead

Christianity is the only religion whose founder rose from the dead and was seen by hundreds of eyewitnesses. Jesus' resurrection is the ultimate proof of his deity and his identification as the promised Messiah of the Old Testament (Rom. 1:1–4). Even skeptical historians who deny Jesus to be the Son of God cannot escape the historical fact that three days after Jesus was buried his tomb was empty.

Gary Habermas, professor at Liberty University and expert of the resurrection of Christ, estimates that 75 percent of historical scholars (both Christian and non-Christian) believe that Jesus' tomb was empty three days after his crucifixion. In other words, the historical evidence for the empty tomb is very strong. On top of that, the belief that Jesus rose from the dead is the best explanation for what happened in the weeks following Jesus' death. The transformation of a ragtag group of terrified followers into a powerful movement attracting thousands who proclaimed the resurrection of a crucified criminal can only logically be explained by the fact that Jesus rose again.

The Gospel accounts of Jesus' resurrection have a number of features that lead many scholars to consider them reliable. First, the initial eyewitnesses of Jesus after his resurrection were women (Matt. 28:5–7). In the culture at that time the testimony of a woman was considered to be worth only half of a man's. So if you were inventing the resurrection story, you would never include women as the first eyewitnesses. You would perhaps write civil authorities or religious experts into the story as the first eyewitnesses. Since women are, in fact, credited with being the first to see Jesus, the Gospel accounts are more likely accurate. Second, when the women told Jesus' disciples that the tomb was empty and that they had seen Jesus, the disciples didn't believe them at first (Lk. 24:11). This shows that the disciples were not expecting Jesus to rise from the dead. Third, some critics believe that the accounts of Jesus' life and resurrection are legends rather than factual history. However, the examples we have of legends arising in antiquity (the ancient world) all demonstrate that such legends take hundreds of years to emerge. The written accounts on which the Gospels are based, however, began to be written within just a few years of Jesus' life, clearly not enough time for legends to arise. So anyone who wants to argue that the Gospels are legends is arguing against the way history works.

By challenging unbelievers with these claims and facts of Jesus, you put before them the most important question any person has to answer: What will you do with Jesus? This is the goal of apologetics—getting unbelievers to face up to the claims of Jesus and show that Jesus is who he claimed to be and can save them from the sin which condemns them.

Show the Glory and Rationality of the Christian Faith

When someone rejects the Christian faith, he rejects a worldview that answers the deep yearnings of the human heart and the difficult questions of the human condition. The reason for this is that the Christian faith is centered in a person, not an ideal or an abstract idea. Because Jesus is the center of Christianity, all the glory of the divine Son of God is behind the answers Christianity gives. Only the Christian worldview truly makes sense of the following questions:

First, why am I here? What is my purpose? Each worldview, belief system, and religion has an answer for these questions. Let's take one, atheistic naturalism (AN), and show how it fails to answer these questions with any degree of satisfaction. Atheistic naturalism denies the existence of God and believes that all questions can be answered by science because the physical world is all that exists.

The answer AN gives to the first question is that we are here because the random forces of natural selection, guided by blind chance and time, just happened to produce this universe and everything in it. Since evolution is a blind process, there cannot be *purpose*, because purpose implies intelligence. There is no intelligence or design in the universe, so whatever happens to be, just is. There can be no purpose or meaning to life. We are here for nothing more than survival.

In contrast, the Christian worldview tells us that we are a special creation by a personal God who not only designed this universe for the purpose of human life but has communicated purpose to us in his Word. Our purpose, as human beings made in God's image, is to bring God glory. This other-focused purpose frees us from thinking we are the center of the universe. Life has inherent meaning because of God's design in creation.

There is a universal longing for purpose and meaning in every person. Even when a person believes in AN, he longs for his life to have meaning. When talking to an adherent of AN, push the issue of meaning and purpose. Show how AN cannot provide purpose or meaning, and in fact makes it impossible. Only in the Christian worldview can a person find meaning.

Second, who am I? Where did we come from? In AN, the individual is an accident of nature. He is nothing more than the sum total of his genes. He is no different from animals, and therefore has no more significance than a snail on the sidewalk. Ultimately AN has no answer for the origins of life. The universe came about by the Big Bang, but no one knows from where the original elements came.

In contrast, Christianity says we are unique among all created things. We are made in God's image, made to know him, and made to reflect his glory. This provides us with an identity directly related to the divine God. Our identity does not consist of our performance, failures, successes, family, anything we do, or what is done to us. Since God is our creator and sovereign, we are not our own. We belong to God and owe him our allegiance. Only in acknowledging this can we find our true selves and find joy.

Third, what is wrong with the world? Why is there evil and suffering? Those who hold the AN worldview face a real crisis with these questions. If evolution is true, and we are just the sum total of our genes, and life is guided by blind chance, and there is no meaning in the universe, then there is nothing wrong with this world. The world is exactly the way it is supposed to be, with all the murder, rape, genocide, slavery, human trafficking, theft, hatred, cancer, disease, poverty, tsunamis, hurricanes, tornados, earthquakes, and so on. Yet, atheists cannot escape the urge to see many of the things mentioned to be wrong, or in need of correction. They are often deeply concerned with human suffering, even though they are inconsistent in their concern. In the AN worldview, whatever happens in this world is what is supposed to happen. Whatever happens is simply the result of natural selection. Ultimately, this is a very dissatisfying conclusion for most people, who want there to be meaning in suffering.

The Christian faith teaches that the world is *not* the way it is supposed to be. God created the world perfect, with no death or sin. Since the fall of Adam and Eve into sin, however, the world is under the curse of sin. Nothing in the universe is as it should be, and the whole creation groans for the day when Christ will transform it (Rom. 8:22–23). Evil resides in the human heart, and anyone is capable of evil. God is sovereign over all events, so nothing happens outside God's control. We suffer in this lifetime, but God has saved us from ultimate suffering by the death of his Son, Jesus.

Fourth, where are we going? What is the end of all this? In AN there is no ultimate end or final purpose of life. There is nothing after death. There is no afterlife, so life on this earth will continue without change until the resources of the earth are used up. There is no heaven or hell, so there is no reward for living a good life, and no punishment for those who have done evil. There is no good or evil so whatever you do to be happy is all that matters. There is no real value such as justice because all values are relative. No God will ever judge you, so do what you want with your one life, because after this life is nothing.

The Christian worldview teaches that there is an eternal destiny for each person. This world will soon come to an end, and life in this sin-cursed world will be over. Justice matters in this life, and in the end, God will bring justice. Every evildoer will be punished, and those who have been saved by divine grace will enjoy eternal bliss with God. Every desire that has been frustrated in this life will be satisfied for believers in the next life. As C. S. Lewis wrote, "If we find ourselves with a desire that nothing in this world can satisfy, the most probable explanation is that we were made for another world."[21]

Conclusion

The centrality of Jesus in apologetics and evangelism cannot be emphasized enough. There is nothing more powerful in dismantling the unbeliever's opposition to Christianity than to have him discover that the gospel is not about keeping a moral code, or attaining some enlightenment, but rather about meeting a person. God has provided overwhelming historical evidence for what we believe about Jesus. This lesson touched on some of that evidence, although this topic can only be explored in depth in other volumes. For now, what has been presented is a good start for a student to learn and have ready when challenged by an unbeliever.

We want to develop a Jesus-oriented apologetic, where we are always trying to work Jesus into the conversation. The person and work of Jesus are the central issues in the gospel, so the sooner we can clear away obstacles and talk about Jesus, the sooner we can get to the heart of the issue. The more we learn how Jesus answers the questions of the human heart, the more we will be able to present a compelling, attractive understanding of the gospel that appeals to the unbeliever's awareness of his separation from God. Even when people still have intellectual objections to the gospel, if they find Jesus to be a gentle Savior and Shepherd, they will be drawn to him.

Chapter Seven

Sharing the Gospel Effectively

The guest speaker in college chapel that day was winsome and engaging. He told interesting stories of his years in professional sports that had many students' eyes glued to the stage. He didn't use much Scripture, but was sharing good advice, funny anecdotes, and helpful principles. As he wrapped up his message, he asked for every head to be bowed, and eyes to be closed. He began to issue an invitation to the students with earnest, heartfelt urgency.

"Have you ever surrendered to Christ? Have you committed your life to him? Is Jesus on the throne of your life right now? If you would like to give your life fully to Christ, raise your hand!"

It was a compelling invitation, and yet as I looked up—because, you know, as a professor, I wanted to be "helpful" in case I was called upon to counsel and pray with students—I noticed widespread confusion in the student body. Students were looking up and around, whispering to one another with puzzled looks on their faces. Some were tentatively raising their hands, only to lower them again as he proceeded to elaborate on his call for a response.

Their perplexity was justified, for I, too, was unsure of the exact intent of the invitation. Was he inviting unbelieving students (yes, we have those at Bible college) to be saved? Was he challenging Christian students who had slipped into sin or apathy to renew their fervor for God? What exactly was the point of all this?

In the end, many students walked away from chapel that day buzzing. Some gushed about the humor, and some about his sports career, but most wondered what his purpose was in the invitation.

This is a common scenario in many churches and Christian institutions. Vague, incomplete, and confusing presentations of the gospel abound. In an attempt to creatively communicate the message of the gospel, many people resort to generic religious phrases or misleading metaphors. The net result is that confusion abounds about what the message of the gospel actually is. Some who respond to a weak gospel invitation and do not understand what they are doing in their response believe themselves to be Christian, when in reality they are not. Others never think of salvation in specific, biblical terms, and so are confused about what actually happened to them. Most of these people will perpetuate further confusion regarding the gospel when they try to share it with others. We must never assume our hearers know what is meant by "the gospel," since much confusion abounds regarding the term.

Because our ultimate goal in apologetics is to lead people to a saving knowledge of Jesus Christ, it is critical that we know how to share the good news of the gospel accurately, specifically, and effectively. This chapter simplifies the message of the gospel, so that we will be able to proclaim it with confidence.

Use Biblical Terms

One of the most obvious problems with the vague descriptions of salvation and the gospel often used among Christians is that they do not appear in the very source of our knowledge of the gospel, the Bible. It would seem to make sense that we ought to draw not only the grand, theological ideas about the nature of salvation from Scripture, but also the terminology we use to communicate it.

When we see the ministry of Jesus introduced in the Gospels, his message is simple: "repent and believe in the gospel" (Mk. 1:15). These twin concepts encapsulate the proper response to the gospel that God requires in order to be saved. Repentance and faith are often portrayed as two sides of the same coin. That is, they are distinct but inseparable. True repentance is turning away from sin that is only caused by a recognition that only Jesus is able to forgive. True faith happens only when a person places all her faith in the person of Jesus Christ after seeing a true picture of her sinfulness.

Rather than some vague sense of needing to surrender, commit, give, or dedicate their lives to Christ, when the gospel is presented using biblical terms, the call to acknowledge guilt and turn away from sin is clear and simple. In addition, the biblical terms remind us that salvation is not a "decision" that a person makes based on information he did not know previously. By calling for repentance, the apologist or evangelist is proclaiming the truth of the unbeliever's condition in hope that the Holy Spirit will bring conviction of sin and belief that Jesus is the only solution. By calling for faith in Christ, he is calling on the unbeliever to cast all his hope for eternal life on Jesus.

The simplicity and clarity of the terms "repent" and "believe" are powerful because they minimize confusion about what makes a person reconciled to God. They also place emphasis on a person's primary need—being reconciled to God. While salvation does many things—restores hope, provides peace, transforms families, relieves fear, and gives meaning and purpose—the primary need of every person is to find reconciliation with God.

Focus on Sin and Guilt

Salvation through Christ is necessary because of human guilt. While people come to Christ for many reasons, we always want to emphasize that every person needs to be reconciled because of their sin, which brings guilt. This can be difficult to communicate when the unbeliever has more immediate concerns on her mind. If her marriage is failing, or if she is overcome with anxiety over a medical diagnosis, she may be interested in talking about Jesus because subconsciously she is hoping that praying to him may fix her problem.

A man who is out of work or feeling guilty for not being a good father may be willing to pray to God, not because he sees his need for forgiveness from sin but because he wants God to get him a job or relieve the regret he has over the lost time with his children. A teenager may have broken the law or done something about which her parents will be angry, and so will pray a prayer without any sense of her greater guilt before God.

When unbelievers express these feelings, we should not brush them aside to get right to their guilt before God. God may be using anxiety or regret to bring them to a place of openness to the gospel. We should listen and encourage with the truths of Christ, showing them that their immediate problem is part of a larger consequence of living in a sin-cursed world.

While we want to tell them that God can help them with the immediate problem, we never want to tell them that God will necessarily fix their problems if they would simply repent and believe. The truth is, we don't know what God will do about those problems if they believe.

Rather, we should direct their attention to Jesus as the person who not only has the power to solve their problems, but to do more than that—secure their eternal destiny by reconciling them to God. But we must also emphasize that God may leave their circumstances the way they are. Believing in Christ means accepting Jesus unconditionally. If the emphasis is placed on their sin and guilt, and unbelievers are convicted and repentant, then they will be willing to believe regardless of their circumstances.

Emphasize the Love of God in Christ

In addition to a focus on the person's sin and guilt, we want to present the good news of the gospel as the Bible does, with an emphasis on the incredible love of God for the sinner. The Bible never offers the gospel merely as an escape from wrath, but also an embrace by a loving, heavenly Father whose love overcomes our estrangement and rebellion. In the story of the prodigal son, the father runs to his son, throws his arms around him, kisses him, and immediately sets about removing his shame and clothing him with fine garments. He orders prime rib, steaks, and filet mignon, and commands a celebration to begin (Lk. 15:20–24). This story reminds us of the deep love God has for unbelievers, and his desire to reconcile the sinner to himself.

When an unbeliever is reconciled to God, he is not given a merely neutral existence. Rather, he is welcomed into a family, participates in a covenant that is entirely for his benefit, becomes an ambassador, and becomes a part of a community. These bless-ings of salvation often meet the social, emotional, and spiritual needs that naturally arise when a person is estranged from God. Someone who has been left lonely and unconnected by the bro-kenness of the world will find his welcome as a beloved child to be comforting. Likewise, someone that has no friendships or support may be surprised by the new community of faith he finds in a church. Someone who has been abandoned, betrayed, and taken advantage of will find a covenant relationship with God that cannot be broken to be a source of security and safety.

How can we communicate that God loves the unbeliever? We need to remind them that God loves them, not because they are deserving of that love and good enough, but because God's very nature is to love sacrificially those who don't deserve it. He loves so abundantly and sacrificially that he gave his own Son to die, so that guilty sinners can be reconciled to him.

Emphasize Grace Instead of Merit

Not long ago I was talking with Warren, the owner of an inn where I stay on occasion. We'd had the chance to talk about his spiritual condition once before, and this time he was more interested than ever to talk about Christ. He seemed to want to be sure that he was in good standing with God, and not missing anything in his thoughts about God. It became obvious that he had no objections to what I was saying about the love of God, the death and resurrection of Christ, and his own guilt before God. He accepted all that without question.

After asking questions for almost half an hour to see why he was reluctant to put his faith in Christ, it became clear that he struggled to understand the concept of grace. He finally asked the question that many religious people harbor when confronted with God's grace: "What motivation is there to do good and live a moral life if I don't have to earn my place with God?" In other words, faced with the free gift of salvation, he balked because he wanted his good works to count for something!

We often encounter two responses to the message of salvation by God's grace through faith. The first is an inability (at first) to even comprehend the idea. For some, the idea of merit (earning favor with God) is so deeply ingrained that they cannot understand that reconciliation with God happens purely by grace. The second reaction is the one Warren exhibited; when a sense of self-righteousness is strong enough, some people will bristle at the thought that none of their good works count for anything with God. They don't want to be reconciled by grace; they want their efforts to be acknowledged and rewarded!

What can we do in such cases? I have found analogies to help unbelievers understand grace. The relationship of a husband to a wife, or parents to their children, helps. I asked Warren, "What would you think if I made it clear to my wife or kids that they had to earn my love? What if I told them that I would be happy to love them if they deserved it? Most of us would rightly be appalled. A healthy relationship is such where love is given freely and unconditionally. The hope is that such a relationship would motivate reciprocal love, consideration, and kindness." This analogy seemed to help him understand that good works should be considered an expression of gratitude or worship, and not a way to earn merit with God.

Bringing It All Together

As you present the gospel clearly, one of two things will happen: Either the person will indicate that she has reached her limit of listening, or she will indicate a desire to know what comes next. She may show that she has reached her limit by saying, "I don't want to talk about this anymore," or "I'll have to think about that, but for now I don't believe that." She may display body language that is more defensive or simply, less open.

In such cases we must remember that our trust is in the Holy Spirit's conviction of sin and drawing to Christ. If a person is not ready to repent and believe, we can trust the sovereignty of God to use what progress we have made in her life. We don't have to force a person to pray a prayer or confess Christ out of the personal pressure we apply to them. The person may simply not be ready to become a follower of Christ. We should always conclude such a conversation with encouragement to read the Gospels and an invitation to continue the conversation at some point. Converted lesbian, feminist-turned-pastor's-wife Rosaria Butterfield tells how the couple who led her to Christ opened up their home and invited her to dinner regularly for more than a year until she put her faith in Christ. As much as the verbal testimony, the hospitality of this pastor and his wife was what led to her salvation. [22]

What if your conversation partner seems open to hearing more after you have clearly presented the gospel, and she has indicated that she believes the truths of the gospel? A gentle yet compelling approach might be to ask, "Is there anything keeping you from trusting in Jesus Christ right now?" This question is effective, because it brings to light any lingering obstacles or questions in the heart before the unbeliever is invited to call upon God for salvation. If we rush her into a prayer or call to believe, she may do so reluctantly or without real repentance and faith. We always want to be as sure as we can that the person has come under conviction of sin and is ready to call upon the name of the Lord out of the Spirit's work in her heart.

If she affirms her desire to repent and believe, she may need assistance to know what to do. Not everyone needs specific help at this point. Some people who are overcome by their guilt and need of Christ will naturally cry out to God in repentance and belief. Others, however, need to have someone clarify what she is doing in calling upon God for salvation. Explain that she should tell God herself that she is a sinner who is guilty before him, and to ask Jesus to save her from her sin. She should express belief that Jesus is the only way to be made right with God. She can also thank God for saving her, forgiving her sin, and making her his child.

Some evangelists recommend having the unbeliever pray out loud after them, phrase by phrase. While there is nothing necessarily wrong with this, encouraging the person to pray out loud in their own words after you have given instruction is usually better. It allows the person to express for herself her guilt and belief in Christ. Every person feels the weight of their sin differently and so needs to have the opportunity to express their repentance in personal terms. A good example of the variety of ways sin condemns, binds, and kills us can be found in Psalm 107. In this psalm, unbelievers are variously described as lost, imprisoned in sin, dying from the illness of sin, and in great physical danger. I believe this demonstrates the various ways people identify what is wrong in their lives when they come to the point of crying out to the Lord for his deliverance and healing, as recounted in this psalm. Therefore, not everyone will use the same exact words as they repent and call upon Jesus to save them. The important elements are simply repentance and an expression of belief (Rom. 10:9–10).

Conclusion

It is critical that when we invite someone to respond in faith to the message of the gospel, we are clear about what the gospel is. By describing the elements of the message of Jesus thoroughly, we lessen considerably the chance that the unbeliever will be confused about what the Holy Spirit is drawing him toward. This is the final step in our apologetic and should be presented as clearly as possible.

Chapter Eight

Strategies for Effective Apologetic Encounters

"But what if the person asks me a question I can't answer? How do I know where to go with the conversation? What if my mind goes blank?"

The woman who asked these questions had just sat through one of my weekend conferences, and yet felt at a loss as she contemplated sharing the truth of the gospel with her friends and coworkers in the coming week.

Her predicament is a common one. We can learn lots of things about apologetics, feel very confident in the middle of an apologetics conference, and yet seemingly forget everything we have learned the moment we come face-to-face with real people.

Part of the answer is to find reassurance that we know more than we think we do—if we have been discipled under sound preaching in our local church, or if we have spent time studying how to give an answer. This is where the historic creeds and confessions of the Christian church can be helpful. Very few people have the ability to spontaneously speak on any topic related to belief, unbelief, religion, and the like. Most of us need an occasion or a conversation to jog our memory of what we know. This is where we need these reminders that Jesus gave his disciples before he ascended to the Father:

- We have the Spirit of truth living in us (Jn. 14:17).
- The Spirit brings to mind what we have previously learned (Jn. 14:26).
- The Spirit will declare the truth to us (Jn. 16:13–15).
- All authority in heaven and earth belongs to Jesus (Matt. 28:18).
- Jesus is with us at all times (Matt. 28:20).

We need to remember that the Holy Spirit who dwells in believers is the one who will bring to mind what we have forgotten in our short-term memory. The Spirit is the one who will give us words to say when we don't know on our own. While we should prepare to engage all manners of unbelief, we can never remember everything, nor can we always be knowledgeable about every belief system.

Once we establish the Holy Spirit as the foundation for our apologetic, we can begin to talk about specific tactics that can be used to expose the unbeliever's presuppositions and worldview. These strategies provide us with multiple ways to challenge unbelief and present the truth of the gospel. When to use which one is entirely dependent on the nature of the encounter with the unbeliever, the extent of the Christian's knowledge and ability to recognize contradictions and irrationality, and the interest or antagonism of the unbeliever. These tactics can be used by the average Christian to make progress in a gospel conversation with any unbeliever she may encounter.

Strategies

First, listen for mistaken beliefs. Erroneous ideas come in all shapes and sizes. Sometimes a person will quote a statistic that you don't know is true or not. Other times someone may make an argument against God using theoretical physics or French philosophy. They may bring up a passage of Scripture that they find objectionable, when you have never studied that passage or heard a good explanation of it. The truth is, you can never be so well versed in every area of human inquiry that you will have a specific answer for all the objections that get thrown at you in an apologetic encounter.

When unbelievers include "facts" in their argument that are new or unfamiliar to you, don't panic. In reality, you don't know whether these "facts" are really true or not; and if they are real facts, they may be taken out of context or misinterpreted. The Christian must automatically challenge any "fact" used to supposedly discredit the truth of the gospel.

Believers need to be reminded that all wisdom rests in Christ and his gospel, so whatever "facts" are wielded against Christianity are misused or mistaken. The Christian must start with the basic presupposition that this is God's world and that everything in it declares his glory (Ps. 19:1–2) and declares it so clearly that unbelievers are without excuse in God's sight. So, although I may not know how to answer the objection raised, I know that there is an answer.

So what should we do if someone argues an idea with which we are unfamiliar or unsure? As we learned in earlier lessons, we should challenge the "fact." We can say something like:

- I've never heard that before, but it doesn't seem right to me. What is the source for your information?

- I don't know anything about that topic (or subject, issue, etc.). How exactly does that, if it is true, discredit the Christian faith?

- I think what you are saying is inaccurate or just plain wrong. I don't have proof or a strong argument right now, but I wouldn't base my unbelief on that if I were you. I will find details or arguments and get back to you.

- I am skeptical of that "fact." That seems pretty far-fetched (or contradicts what we know about real life). Maybe you should be more skeptical of your sources.

These may seem to be direct or even blunt responses, but when we are dealing with ignorance or willful rejection of the truth, sometimes we need to be somewhat forceful with the truth. We dare not let mistaken or erroneous ideas go unchallenged in a discussion, lest we undermine further conversation. For example, if I don't correct mistaken notions about what the Bible is and how it was written and preserved, I undermine my appeal to the Scriptures later, because I will have given the impression that I can't answer challenges to my primary authority.

Second, listen for logical fallacies. To be rational, we must be logical. Logic keeps us from descending into irrationality. For example, everyone can recognize the irrationality of the following statement. "The sun rises in the east; therefore, you should buy me a new car today." The second statement does not logically follow from the first, and the first provides no justification for the second. Logic means that we seek to provide reasons for the beliefs we hold. If our beliefs are not based on sound reasons, then we ought to find sound reasons on which to base them, or conversely, abandon those beliefs.

The Christian's core beliefs are grounded in the revelation of God in his Word. The fact that the Bible says something is justification enough for us to believe it, because of our previous beliefs in its authority, reliability, and self-attestation as God's revelation. We should always seek to believe only what we have good reasons to believe. That eliminates beliefs based on conspiracy theories, wishful thinking, fear, hatred, and a host of other faulty foundations. We dare not commit logical fallacies ourselves if we are going to critique the fallacies of those who reject the truth of the Christian faith.

Unbelievers often commit logical fallacies in their arguments against the gospel. One common fallacy is the disconnect between the evolutionary, materialist view of life and the supposed obligation to be good and love others. Russian philosopher Vladimir Solovyov summarizes it this way: "Man descended from apes, therefore we must love one another."[23] Clearly the first claim in no way logically results in the second (more on logical fallacies in Chapter 9).

Third, listen for implicit bias. Implicit bias is another way of describing subconscious assumptions or unexamined presuppositions. That is, everyone assumes certain things to be true, obvious, and unable to be challenged. Yet many of these biases cannot be shown to be true, and in fact can be shown to be false. For example, some people have a reactive bias that makes them want to do the opposite of what someone else is trying to get them to do, or alternately believe the opposite of what someone is telling them. This bias springs from many sources, but one obvious one is the dislike of being proven wrong. This is one of the reasons the *way* we engage people is so important. If they sense we enjoy proving them to be wrong rather than helping them find truth, we might inflame the reactive bias unnecessarily. The apostle John mentions that Jesus was "full of grace and truth." What a great reminder that our manner is as important as our message.

Another bias that influences our thinking is known as "sunk cost fallacy." If a friend has invested time, money, or reputation in a particular belief, he is less likely to admit the belief is wrong. To do so would be to lose all he has invested in that belief. For example, if someone establishes their reputation as a skeptic, becomes known for his skepticism, and has written a book on it, to admit that he is wrong comes at a high price, and his investment in skepticism has to be considered a waste. This is one of the reasons why the Holy Spirit's conviction is necessary in conversion. Without the Spirit reassuring a person's heart that loss for the sake of Christ is good, no one would ever be willing to do as Paul did—counting everything but the knowledge of Christ as loss.

Fourth, look for positions that would be embarrassing to maintain. Every worldview besides the Christian faith results in logical conclusions that are an embarrassment in a civilized society. For example, an agnostic acquaintance of mine is an avid participant in state politics. He frequently spends time in the state capitol trying to forbid reference to any religious basis in legislation. In other words, he does not want religion to play a part in any laws that are passed. He is a typical example of a secular humanist.

When I bring up the explicitly Christian foundation of Martin Luther King's legacy in the civil-rights movement or William Wilberforce's battle to end the slave trade in England, however, he becomes uncomfortable. He knows that if he is to be consistent with his principle, he would have to condemn the Christian foundations for these movements. But to do so would be to say that it would have been better to wait for secular activists to resist slavery. This is a claim no one wants to make, because it smacks of racism—a racism that is condemned in Scripture, but not consistently so from a secular humanist standpoint.

Fifth, capitalize on universally held values (justice, opposition to trafficking, abuse, etc.). Many people today who deny the existence of objective morality feel very passionately about certain moral and social issues without realizing the contradiction. They may believe that any sexual choice is perfectly acceptable (as long as there is consent), but become animated about issues of justice, equality, racism, human trafficking, and more (as they should!).

Whenever someone criticizes Christianity for its call to sexual purity, I often ask questions that get to the heart of their morality. The conversation will develop something like this:

> Mark: So, you believe that everyone should be able to enjoy whatever sexual practices that make them happy?
>
> Unbeliever: Yes, every person should be able to have their own morality and do as they please.
>
> M: Is that because there is no absolute morality?
>
> U: Yes, that is correct. Morality is relative to each person's conscience.
>
> M: So, if someone wants to traffic people as sex slaves, they have the right to do that?
>
> U: No! Of course not!

M: But why not? Didn't you say morality is relative?

U: Yes, but human trafficking is obviously wrong. No one gets to make that choice.

M: But how do you exclude that activity from your rule?

U: Because an act that involves others must be by consent.

M: But where do you get consent? It seems you have pulled that moral rule out of thin air. You have provided no basis for requiring that people consent to what involves them. That makes sense in a Christian worldview where each person is made in the image of God and is afforded dignity as a result. But how do you argue for that in your worldview? And besides, don't those who traffic other human beings often beat, bully, and threaten them into consent? Don't they get their slaves to say they are choosing this life when they are questioned by authorities? If we reduce consent to merely verbally affirmed nonresistance, we have no way to resist someone who is exploiting another person.

You can see, in this fictional exchange, that there are certain topics related to justice and human dignity that not many people want to oppose publicly because of the near-universal agreement that such things are wrong. It is rather easy to show that these issues only make sense in a Christian worldview.

Sixth, identify assertions when arguments are called for. Another common mistake we make when arguing a point is that . . . we don't actually argue a point! To argue for something is to make logical inferences from two or more truths. Quite often, however, we make assertions rather than present arguments. To assert something is simply to state it without any supporting justification. For example, to say "Christians believe the Bible because they can't cope with the reality of life and need a crutch on which to rest" is only an assertion if no supporting statements are given that prove that it is true.

Sometimes when we are defending the Christian faith our opponent will make a statement such as the one above. If we don't recognize it for what it is—a mere assertion—we will often feel helpless to respond. The reason is that an assertion made without any supporting arguments feels like an unimpeachable truth. That is, it comes across with the force of a universally accepted law. But it is not. Until a statement is supported by arguments it is actually nothing more than a wisp of smoke to be waved away. And mere assertion appears in apologetic conversations frequently!

Here are some examples of assertions that need to be challenged:

- Science has disproved the Bible.
- All religions are the same.
- There is no proof whatsoever for God.
- Christianity is bad for the world.
- We don't know what the original manuscripts of the New Testament said.

As you can see, these statements seem very intimidating, because they are stated in such a decisive fashion. But they are nothing more than unsupported assertions. We should apply our questions from Chapter 5 whenever anyone tries to get away with such statements.

Seventh, pursue wisely those who wish to avoid conversation on spiritual issues. Sometimes in your efforts to engage people with the gospel, you encounter disinterest or resistance to conversation about spiritual topics. But even if someone tells you directly, "I don't like to talk about religion," it doesn't mean that the conversation is automatically over. I usually try at least one more strategy if this happens. I will ask, "Oh really? Why?" in the most winsome way possible. That is, sometimes people attempt to shut down the conversation to avoid admitting the reason they don't want to talk about spiritual issues.

By asking why, you may find that the answer relates to previous bad experiences with Christians, or alternately, a loss that has caused them to question the goodness of God in a broken world. By pressing the issue just a bit, you may uncover an openness to further conversation. If the person declines to answer, however, I don't continue to pursue the conversation. I don't want to come across as pushy or aggressive. I will simply pray for her and hope to meet again.

Conclusion

Hopefully these strategies provide more clarity and give more tools for effective conversations. Much of it is intuitive. That is, if I keep in mind the command to give an answer with gentleness and respect (1 Pet. 3:15), I will strive to clear objections, so that I can talk about Jesus without being annoying. I will listen to what the unbeliever is saying and how she is answering my questions. I will look for ways to incorporate these strategies in order to get to the root of her objections. I will seek to reveal the inconsistencies and irrationality of her worldview and the foundation on which it rests. We should think of ourselves as skilled surgeons using well-crafted instruments, as opposed to thugs with swords looking for a fight.

Remember, as you are employing these strategies, you are tearing down the intellectual and emotional strongholds that the unbeliever has built up over time. These strategies give you various ways to challenge the objections, assumptions, and mistaken notions accumulated over time. Effective engagement requires patience and the insight of the Holy Spirit. Because the Spirit dwells inside us and because we have the divinely revealed Word of God, we can be used by God for the planting and watering of gospel seeds in the lives of those who don't know Christ.

Chapter Nine

Basic Logic for Apologetics

"Christianity is just not logical!"
A friend of mine who serves in Spain began to encounter this objection when he tried to talk about faith in Jesus Christ. He wrote to me and asked how he could respond. To commit your life to something that is illogical is a serious charge. If Christianity is truly illogical it calls into question how we can expect modern people to believe it. Even more, it raises the question of how we can believe it ourselves. Is the gospel truly against logic?

The answer lies in the nature of logic itself. Logic is one of the powerful tools of apologetics. Logic has the power to expose contradictions in both our own thoughts and in the worldviews of unbelievers. Christians are often viewed as illogical and irrational by unbelievers who put great emphasis on rationality, logic, and scientific precision. While it is true that Christians can be illogical and irrational, the Christian faith is neither of these things. The Christian faith is the only belief system that truly reflects the nature of the world and truth as it is. All other belief systems are denials or distortions of the truth. Laws of logic are a reflection of the character of God himself, and so apart from God the unbeliever cannot account for logic.

One of the most powerful ways to defend the Christian faith is to identify and refute logical fallacies in the objections raised against the Christian faith. This requires, first of all, that our own reasoning is marked by true and sound thought. In this chapter we will learn how logic can help us see through the false beliefs of unbelievers we meet.

Logic is the art and science of reasoning well. More formally, it is "the study of the methods by which the conclusion is proved beyond all doubt."[24] In other words, logic is what distinguishes between what is not true, what may be true, and what is necessarily true, given the facts. Logic helps us avoid contradiction and irrationality. It also keeps us from allowing incidental or unimportant factors from interfering with our quest for the truth. For example, whether I like something or not, if it is true, I should believe it. Whether or not I like the person who is telling me a fact, if the fact logically follows from the evidence, I should believe it. To reject a truth on the basis of these factors would be illogical. There are many such mistakes we can make in our thinking, and we typically call them logical fallacies.

Logical Fallacies

Errors in the structure of logical arguments are called formal fallacies. For the sake of brevity, we don't cover them in this book. Rather we move on to the most common mistakes in informal logic known as logical fallacies. These are flaws in reasoning that superficially seem to be sound, but upon examination are found to be false. The power of logical fallacies is that even after they have been shown to be flawed, they still retain their power to convince because they are often emotionally satisfying.

For example, many Christians believe the following statement to be true, even though it is a fallacy, because it gives them confidence: "Millions of people around the world and throughout history have found peace and hope in Jesus, therefore he must be the way to salvation." While it is true that becoming a follower of Christ gives peace, that truth does not prove Christianity true. People feel a sense of peace through many means—other religions, no religion, meditation, addictive substances, catching a great wave, or a hike in the woods. This fallacy is called *appeal to popularity*, an argument based on what a large number of people think or believe. It reminds us that nothing is ever true just because it is popular or the majority position.

What follows is a short list of some popular logical fallacies that both believers and unbelievers tend to use in support of or opposition to the Christian faith. I will explain each one, show examples of how both groups argue the fallacy, and then show what is wrong with both.[25] This exercise should help us see that we need to present our reasons for what we believe in true and valid ways. Many of these fallacies have Latin names (*post hoc, ad hominem, tu quoque*), but for the sake of simplicity I have listed their common English names.

Appeal to Authority

Here, a claim is defended or advanced on the basis of those who believe it. While we may appeal to the arguments of experts in a particular field, just because recognized experts advocate or deny a position does not make it true or false.

How Christians do this:

"Einstein believed in a higher being, and he was the smartest man in the twentieth century, so you should, too."

"Billy Graham spoke to more people than any other evangelist in history, and everywhere he went people were converted, so that shows that the gospel is the truth for every person in the world."

How unbelievers do this:

"Richard Dawkins has said that ninety-three percent of members of the National Academy of Science do not believe in God, so it is not reasonable to believe in God."

"Bart Ehrman is a *New York Times* bestselling author, a world-renowned professor at the University of North Carolina, and a graduate of Moody Bible Institute, and he says the manuscripts of the New Testament were corrupted, so it must be true."

This is a fallacy because:

Nothing is ever true because of who said it—except when God says it. Therefore, we should learn the actual argument of the authority and use it to answer objections.

Personal Attack

People employing this fallacy ignore the argument and criticize its author. Accusing the other person of being unreliable, ignorant, or lacking expertise says nothing about the validity of her argument, but it can have a strong emotional impact on listeners.

How Christians do this:

"Mormonism cannot be true. Look at the life and crimes of Joseph Smith!"

"How do you *know* evolution is the way the world came about? Are *you* a scientist?

"Bill Nye only has an undergraduate degree in engineering; therefore, he doesn't know anything about biology or cosmology."

How unbelievers do this:

"Ken Ham only has an undergraduate degree in applied science, so what could he know about advanced science?"

"If Christianity was true, then Christians would not be such hateful, bigoted, racist people."

"The disciples were uneducated fishermen, so their 'eyewitness testimony' about Jesus' resurrection was nothing more than hallucination and superstition."

This is a fallacy because:

It is a form of dishonesty. It distracts from the real issue at hand by focusing on something that has nothing to do with the argument, *whether it is true or false.*

False Cause

This involves attributing a cause to an event or idea that is not the actual cause. Just because it rains every time you bring Sally with you on a picnic does not mean that Sally causes the rain. Just because your favorite baseball team wins whenever you are in your lucky chair, wearing your lucky socks, and eating pretzels does not mean that you are causing the wins with your actions.

How Christians do this:

"Attending public school makes teens more likely to walk away from their faith in college."

"This nation started going downhill when prayer and Bible reading were taken out of schools."

"The reason crime is on the rise is because people have stopped going to church."

How unbelievers do this:

"As church attendance falls, violent crime declines; therefore, the faster we get rid of superstitious notions of God, the more peaceful our society will become."

"Schools that teach children that they are good, and not sinners, have lower rates of failure."

"Science flies you to the moon; religion flies you into buildings"—physicist Victor Stenger[26]

This is a fallacy because:

These arguments attribute a cause to a state of affairs without demonstrating that it truly is the reason. Only when we can demonstrate definitely that one thing caused another should we link cause and effect.

Red Herring

In this instance, an argument seems to support a person's position, but in reality, has nothing to do with the question at hand.

The name of this fallacy is derived from the practice of dragging a bag of red herrings across a scent trail, so that dogs would be distracted and lose the scent. When the question at hand is ignored and a related idea is argued instead, a red herring has been committed. This is a difficult fallacy to spot. We must always fight mental confusion and drift to maintain clarity on what the real issue is.

How Christians do this:

"It doesn't matter that there are so many religions in the world. Christianity is still the truth. You don't have to eat all the different kinds of cereal at the grocery store to have a favorite."

"If the Bible is not true, then you must be saying that my grandparents were wasting their time when they read a Bible verse each day of their lives."

How unbelievers do this:

"How can Christianity be true when there are so many more ways that the church could be helping the homeless?"

"I know God is not real, because I asked him to show himself to me in some way and he didn't."

This is a fallacy because:

The reason for one's position or belief has nothing to do with the belief itself. As with the previous fallacy, we are seeking to show a necessary connection.

False Dilemma

Only two choices are offered when, in fact, there are more options available. Almost always one option is too distasteful to accept, so the listener is forced into a choice he does not want to make.

How Christians do this:

"Ask Jesus to be your Savior right here, right now, regardless of your questions and objections, or you can count on the fact that you will never get into heaven."

"Either you believe in a literal twenty-four-hour, six-day creation, or you cannot become a Christian."

How unbelievers do this:

"Either you believe in science and reject religion, or you must remain in blind superstition and reject modern science."

"Either God is not all-powerful, or he is not all-loving. If God were all-loving, he would want to rid the world of evil. If he were all-powerful, he would be able to get rid of evil in the world. But there is evil in the world, so either God is not all-powerful or not all-loving."

This is a fallacy because:

There are often in reality more choices available than the two presented by the person guilty of this fallacy.

Hasty (or Unwarranted) Generalization

With this type of fallacy, a conclusion about everything of a particular kind is based on one or a few examples. For example, when we judge all car salesmen based on our experience with one or two of them, we commit hasty generalization. We tend to believe that every individual person, thing, or idea is just like the few we have encountered, heard about, or read about online.

How Christians do this:

"Atheists are dangerous and immoral people. I know; my neighbor is an atheist, and he has skull tattoos and yells obscenities at his live-in girlfriend."

"Muslims will never listen to the gospel. Look at how they persecute Christians around the world."

"Nobody wants to hear the gospel anymore. I have tried witnessing to my coworkers, and they just shut me down and refuse to talk to me about God."

How unbelievers do this:

"Christians are dangerous to society. That last shooting was carried out by someone who went to church."

"Churches are all about guilting people into giving their money in exchange for heaven. I visited a church once that took two offerings in one day and the pastor was preaching on money."

This is a fallacy because:

Neither our personal experiences nor a few examples necessarily represent everything in that class of events or people. We should focus on either multiple instances or widely recognized characteristics of a group, if we are going to characterize them a certain way.

Begging the Question

This involves assuming a conclusion to be true without proving it. If I am trying to prove that people have lost the ability to distinguish between right and wrong by citing increased numbers of adulterous affairs and abortions, I am *assuming* adultery and abortion to be wrong, when I should have to *argue* that they are wrong. Even though adultery and abortion *are* wrong, rising incidents of each does not necessarily prove that people have lost the ability to distinguish right and wrong.

How Christians do this:

"I believe the Bible is the Word of God because I just know it to be so."

"Evolution cannot explain the origin of life on earth, because it is not true."

How unbelievers do this:

"Science has disproved the existence of God because there is no scientific evidence for God."

"Jesus cannot be the only way to be reconciled to God, because that would mean all other religions are wrong and most of the world would be condemned."

This is a fallacy because:

Our conclusions should be proven by our arguments, not assumed by them.

Faulty Analogy

We do this by making comparisons between two things that are not similar. An analogy allows us to explain one thing by comparison to another. But every analogy breaks down at some point, and some things bear no similarity with other things. If I compare the gentleness of a mother with her baby to a nuclear explosion, there is little chance that the analogy will be helpful in any way.

How Christians do this:

"The Trinity is like an apple (or an egg, or water, or a three-leaf clover)."

"If a person is spiritually dead then I won't bother sharing the gospel with him, because dead people don't hear you when you talk."

How unbelievers do this:

"Christians used the Bible to support slavery and they were clearly wrong, so when they use the Bible to condemn homosexuality, we can clearly see they are wrongly using the Bible again."

"Our genetic code is 'selfish' and blindly strives to reproduce itself for survival."

This is a fallacy because:

An analogy is not an argument, and a poorly chosen one leads to confusion, not clarity. We must compare things that are actually alike to avoid this fallacy.

Equivocation

When a word or phrase is used in more than one sense, or its meaning changes in the middle of an argument, the conversation descends into confusion. If I ask my teenager to clean his room and we have two different ideas of what "clean" means, communication will fail.

How this confusion happens:

Skeptics love to define faith as "belief despite the lack of evidence," but that is not what Christians mean when they use the word. By "faith" a Christian means trust in God's revelation. If a skeptic says, "I have evidence and you have faith," I must correct his erroneous understanding of faith or we will never get anywhere in the discussion.

Similarly, evolutionists often use the word "science," when in fact they believe in *scientism* (the only things that exist are physical objects; natural, not supernatural, forces guide everything apart from a divine intelligence). If we do not expose the difference, we will find ourselves arguing against science, when in fact we have no misgivings about real science.

This is a fallacy because:

Changing the meaning of a word, even slightly, changes the meaning of a proposition—and thus, the argument as a whole.

Hopefully this explanation of several logical fallacies has helped you notice some fallacies in your own thinking, as well as building discernment for identifying them in the arguments of unbelievers. Skill in detecting logical fallacies takes time and much practice. If you are thinking carefully and critically, however, you will begin to spot fallacies and be able to dismantle them, in order to help another person see the truth more clearly.

A Little Note on Logic

Logic is not the final arbiter of all things true, for several reasons. First, flawed and finite people use logic. That means that while logic may help ensure that we arrive at consistency, the premises upon which logical argumentation are built are sometimes disputed. Two rational people can disagree about a premise, because even statements of fact are often values-laden. That is to say, we don't have a God's-eye-view of reality without having to interpret what we see. Our own biases, limitations, and errors can creep into our thinking.

Second, logic flows from the character of God. Logic does not stand over God, and therefore some things will not seem logical, even though they are true. We can have confidence that the Christian faith is logical, because it flows from the character of the all wise God.

Conclusion

So what did I say to my friend in Spain? As we have discussed throughout this book, whenever you don't know what to say, ask a question. My advice was to ask those who claimed that Christianity was not logical, "*How* is Christianity not logical?" There is, in fact, no logical contradiction in Christianity, as we have seen. The fact that it defies human expectations does not make it illogical.

Christians do not need to resort to logical fallacies, because the Christian faith is the summit of wisdom and rationality. To believe and argue logical fallacies demeans and diminishes the true logic of the gospel. Paul states this clearly in 2 Corinthians 4:3–6 (emphasis added), where Jesus is presented as the wisdom of God:

> And even if our gospel is veiled, it is veiled to those who are perishing. In their case the god of this world has blinded the minds of the unbelievers, to keep them from seeing *the light of the gospel of the glory of Christ*, who is the image of God. For what we proclaim is not

> ourselves, but Jesus Christ as Lord, with ourselves as
> your servants for Jesus' sake. For God, who said, "Let
> light shine out of darkness," has shone in our hearts
> to give *the light of the knowledge of the glory of God* in
> the face of Jesus Christ.

Everything pursued by the major cultures of the first-century Western world was found in Christ. The Greeks sought the light of wisdom, Jews sought knowledge, and the Romans sought glory—and each of these is embodied in the message of Jesus. To seek these things apart from Christ is futile, and to claim to have obtained them apart from Christ reveals irrationality and contradiction.

Paul also reminds us that the wisdom of God is wiser than the greatest of "human" wisdom that contradicts it (1 Cor. 1:20–25). This does not mean that unbelievers are not or cannot be brilliant in many areas of human achievement. Some of the brightest scientists, philosophers, engineers, writers, and so on have rejected Christ. It does mean, however, that they can never understand the *why* of the knowledge they possess. They can never know the purpose for which they and their expertise exist. They can never understand the infinitely glorious spiritual realities of God's world until they are transformed by Christ. To make sense of the world they must devise strategies and explanations fraught with logical fallacies. These strategies "work" for them, but they are not the truth. Our prayer is that the Spirit of God will give sight to their blind eyes, enable them to abandon their resistance to the gospel built on their fallacies, and help them to see clearly the wisdom and rationality that is Christ.

Chapter Ten

Practical Apologetics— Review and Practice

"Are you trying to convert me?" The young man looked at me cautiously.

What was I to say? Of course, the end goal of any conversation with an unbeliever is to lead him closer to faith in Christ. But what did *he* mean by "convert"? If he meant "Would I try to force him into an uncomfortable conversation or praying a prayer?" then the answer was no.

The goal of apologetics, if you remember, is always to lead people closer to faith in Jesus Christ. Returning to the metaphor of planting and watering, we always keep in mind that it is God who brings the harvest of salvation. Whether we are the first to sow the seeds of the gospel or if we have the wonderful joy of leading someone to Christ, our goal is to remove obstacles to faith and show them Christ more clearly. We are not simply debating, arguing, or showing off our knowledge.

With that said, if you have read this far and have not been burdened to get out there and actually engage people with the good news of Christ, you have wasted your time reading this book and I have failed in writing it. Unless we are actively seeking and taking advantage of opportunities to talk to unbelievers about the gospel, we have missed the point. What's more is that we have entered a danger zone. Knowledge without loving action in the form of testifying to the truth of Christ does nothing but puff us up with pride (1 Cor. 8:1).

Review

We have covered a lot of ground in the book so far. The concepts that have been learned are significant and somewhat complex. It takes quite a bit of review and practice before they become intuitive and natural. This chapter utilizes a case study to see how well you have absorbed the content of this book so far. After the case study, I provide potentially correct answers for the scenario. Responding to the case study is not so much a science as it is an art. Yet, within the range of approaches, there are right and wrong ways to pursue conversation with the characters.

One of the limitations of a written case study is that the dynamic is a bit artificial. Real apologetic conversations are face-to-face, with give and take as the conversation progresses. The strength of case studies, however, is that they give you time to think how you will respond to the unbeliever's challenge. In a real conversation you have to think quickly, and the time you have to respond to an objection to Christianity may be just a few seconds. This can be intimidating in itself, so a case study provides an opportunity for you to take your time.

Guiding Principles

Apologetic encounters with unbelievers should be guided by the following principles:

1. The goal of apologetics is to present the Christian faith confidently, and with respect for, and gentleness with the unbeliever.

2. Even though you may feel fear, keep going! Fear is a sign you are doing something right.

3. The goal is not to argue with the unbeliever, but to draw him out by asking questions that get to the heart of his worldview.

4. The goal of the conversation is to challenge his objections and answer his questions, so you can present the claims of Christ.

The Game Plan

Here are some of the tactics used when engaging unbelievers:

1. The questions you ask should be focused on getting him to admit or realize on what authority he bases his beliefs.

2. Once he reveals the basis of his beliefs, you should challenge those beliefs.

3. Take his side for the sake of argument and show the consequences of his beliefs when taken to their logical end.

4. Correct mistaken ideas, factual errors, and contradictions.

5. Seek to identify the ways the unbeliever is suppressing the truth of God, so that you can get to the heart of his objections to the gospel.

6. Don't let the unbeliever avoid the implications of his beliefs by changing the subject or jumping to another objection.

7. Weave the Christian answers to the issues you are discussing into your answers to their objections. In other words, as you show the contradiction and irrationality of the unbeliever's worldview, share the Christian worldview as the alternative.

8. As you present the Christian worldview, use Scripture to strengthen your arguments, whether or not the unbeliever values the Bible.

9. Ask questions that push below the surface to the *reason* why he believes what he does. Some common questions include:

   • Why do you believe that?

   • What do you base that on?

   • Where did you get that idea?

   • What makes you think that?

   • What do you mean by that?

   • Can you give me an example of that?

Practice

Case Study #1—Igor, the Skeptical Scientist

You are browsing the science section at Barnes and Noble when you notice a college-age young man thumbing through the popular science section, looking at books by Stephen J. Gould, Richard Dawkins, and Neil de Grasse Tyson. You ask him if he could recommend one of these books, and a conversation ensues.

Igor is a bright young biology student at Millersville University. He is enthusiastic about science, particularly about "the beauty of evolution." He wants to make a career out of studying natural phenomena to unlock the mystery of how they came to evolve over the billions of years.

You mention that you are a Christian, and that you too love science for its ability to explain the complex, but that you see the natural world as a special creation of God. You enjoy science because it reveals not just beauty and complexity in the universe, but also the glory of God. Igor laughs a little and makes it clear that he does not believe in God. Nor does he believe a person can believe in God *and* science. "It's one or the other," he says.

"Science is about the empirical—what can be observed," he states matter-of-factly. "Science cannot demonstrate God because he is not a material being. Science deals with facts, not faith, and the facts all point to the universe as the result of a random, unguided process. Whether God exists or not is irrelevant. The truth is, he cannot be observed, and therefore, he cannot be known.

"Science has brought us the advancements of the twentieth and twenty-first centuries after millennia of superstition and ignorance. To believe in God is to reject all that science has done for us. It is to return us to the Dark Ages and religious tyranny. It threatens us with the specter of new Hitlers and Inquisitions. Science has delivered us from that by making us rational people who can see clearly and reject superstition that harms society.

"If God exists, he is invisible, and we can't really know him. Why would you believe in something you can't see? And if you do, why the Christian God? How do you know Allah or Krishna are not the true gods? What about the Flying Spaghetti Monster, or the Divine Teapot on the far side of Saturn? Why believe the Bible? Science has shown it to be a flawed human product that has been changed thousands of times."

Igor pauses to look you over. "You look normal and sane. Why would you want to read science *and* believe in God? I don't get it."

Responding to Igor

There are a number of ways of responding to Igor. Here are a number of ways to challenge his worldview:

1. You could ask, "*Why* don't you believe in God?"
2. You could ask, "What specifically do you think is the conflict between belief in God and science?"

3. You could agree that science is about observing the empirical. Agreeing with the unbeliever whenever you can shows that you share some common beliefs with him.

4. You could agree that science cannot demonstrate God, because God is not a physical being. However, that also means that science cannot disprove God, because science can only disprove what is in the material realm. Since God is not physical, science cannot render judgment on God's existence or nonexistence.

5. His statement about "fact and faith" is a false dichotomy. Science must employ faith to function, and Christianity deals in historical fact along with faith in God's revelation. You could ask, "Why do you think faith and fact are mutually exclusive?"

6. You could ask, "What facts specifically point to the universe as the result of a random, unguided process?" There are many arguments for seeing beauty as a result of design by a good God. He has already talked about the beauty of the universe, but if everything that exists came about by chance, beauty is purely subjective. There can be no real difference between beauty and ugliness, other than each individual's taste and preference.

7. You could ask why he thinks the existence of God is irrelevant. Christians believe the existence of God is of ultimate importance. It provides meaning in the universe, a basis for morality, and hope for the future.

8. You could challenge him on the idea that we can only know what has been observed by science. How did he come to that conclusion? There are, in fact, many things that we can know without scientific proof. Knowledge

comes from more than just scientific observation. Here are a few examples:

a. The laws of logic are accepted by everyone, yet they cannot be discovered by observing them in nature. They are a logical conclusion, discovered by rational thought, and accepted by faith.

b. Memories are not physical objects, but the result of physical processes. No one would deny that memories are real, can be accurate, and are necessary to function in this world.

c. Whether we like something or not. I know what the taste of garlic is like, and I know whether I like it or not. Both of these experiences count as knowledge, but neither is known by scientific method.

9. You can agree with him that science has, indeed, brought us many advances. Ask him, however, if he is willing to accept science's role in all the pain and suffering brought by science—things like weapons of mass destruction, and medical procedures thought to be good science at one time (like frontal lobotomies for hyper-active children). For every blessing that the modern, scientific world has brought, it has contributed to the death of millions through war, starvation, genocide, torture, and abortion.

10. Disagree that to accept God is to reject science. The simplest way to disprove that is to name the many scientists through the centuries who made advances *because* they believed that this world was designed by a good God who sustained it and created it with regularity. Christians simply refuse to let science go beyond its bounds and determine meaning and values.

11. You could ask why he thinks that science apart from God brought the Western world out of the Dark Ages. It was actually the renewed emphasis on the original languages of the Bible and Latin within the church universities and monasteries that sparked the Renaissance and the Reformation, which brought cultural advancements and societal advances to the world. Christianity was deeply interwoven in that revolution.

12. You could agree that religion does sometimes bring tyranny, as in the case of radical Islam, but that Christianity has historically brought civilization to people who follow it. On the other hand, secular humanism and atheistic regimes such as Communist Russia and China have oppressed the world to a greater degree than any religion ever has. Hitler's Germany, Stalin's Russia, and Mao's China are examples of atheistic tyranny that dwarfs any religious tyranny that has ever existed.

13. You could explain that science is not a neutral endeavor, and that scientists bring their own biases into their work. Scientists often read their preconceived notions into their studies, as is well known among philosophers of science.

14. You could ask him why he thinks that just because something is invisible it shouldn't be believed. As mentioned in point #8 above, there are many things we believe that cannot be observed or studied scientifically.

15. You could point out the uniqueness of the Christian faith compared to other religions and foolish, manmade "deities" such as the Flying Spaghetti Monster, or the Divine Teapot on the far side of Saturn.

a. Christianity is rooted in historical fact, centered on the incarnation of Jesus Christ, for which there is an abundance of evidence.

b. Other religions, such as the Eastern religions, are rooted in myth and not considered historical, even by their adherents.

c. The Christian account of creation, fall, and redemption have more explanatory power when it comes to the significant questions of human existence. Other belief systems cannot consistently account for the meaning and problems of life.

16. You could argue that the Bible's reliability is unparalleled in the religions of the world— or among ancient historical books, for that matter. While sometimes archaeology, science, and history present difficult challenges to the Bible, they do not in any way discredit or disprove the Bible.

17. You could ask how he thinks the Bible has been "changed." Archaeological discoveries such as the Dead Sea Scrolls have clearly demonstrated just the opposite—that the Bible has been remarkably preserved over thousands of years. Copies and translations do not constitute changes to the text of Scripture, but rather demonstrate that despite thousands of manuscripts and translations into many languages, the words of Scripture have been reliably preserved.

Conclusion

Hopefully this case study has helped you begin to think critically about the challenges raised against the Christian faith. You may not have picked up on many of the ways to answer the skeptic in this scenario, but hopefully you came up with a few answers. The truth is, it takes a lot of practice in actual conversations with unbelievers before you begin to see through arguments against Christianity easily.

In the next few chapters, we will shift gears and focus on the core beliefs of the Christian faith, which provide the strength and substance behind a believer's defense of the faith. These chapters will remind us that we do not believe and defend a thin veneer of ideas, but rather a robust, full-bodied theology and worldview that can address any question related to God and this world.

Chapter Eleven

Knowing What You Believe 1—
The Doctrine of Scripture

Many Christians who are interested in evangelism and apologetics make the common mistake of thinking that they don't need to know more than the basic plan of salvation to be a good evangelist. They believe that knowing just a little about Jesus is enough. They may even think that too much knowledge will be a hindrance to effective outreach. As a result, they proclaim a message about Jesus without knowing very many of the details. Consequently, they don't know how to deal with objections to the Christian faith because they are relatively ignorant of the faith they are defending. They are easy prey for an unbeliever who knows even a little of the doctrinal content of the Christian faith and its complexities.

It is no surprise, then, that many Christians avoid interaction with unbelievers because either they have had an unpleasant encounter in which they could not give an answer for an objection raised by an unbeliever, or because they know that they really don't know what they believe. Even worse, they may have serious doubts about some of what they have been taught, because they haven't given the time to study their faith.

Surprisingly, the key to becoming an effective evangelist and apologist is to know the Scriptures and sound doctrine! Knowing what you believe thoroughly provides a sure foundation to confronting the worldviews of others who reject the truth of the gospel. Instead of rushing off to evangelize before they even know what they are proclaiming, Christians would be better served if they would begin to take the time and effort to gain a systematic understanding of their beliefs and the Scriptures on which they are based.

The Relationship between Apologetics and Theology

Theology is, at its heart, the study of God. The word *theology* is the combination of two Greek words, *theos* (God) and *logos* (a word about, or the study of). Christian theology studies all that God has revealed about himself, his creation, and his divine plan. While theology can be understood in its basic form even by children, because it is the study of the infinite, eternal, divine God it can also occupy the greatest minds with its complexity, depth, and beauty.

Apologetics is primarily a biblical and theological endeavor. This surprises many people who think of it first as a philosophical enterprise. While apologetics often deals with the same questions posed by philosophers, and at times incorporates contributions from philosophy, it is not primarily a philosophical activity. Philosophy rejects divine revelation; therefore, it can never provide a true picture of reality or a solution for the redemption of all creation.

Our apologetics, then, must be in agreement with our theology. Even more, it should flow from and be controlled by our theology. Our apologetic method is determined by our theology, not the other way around. If our theology tells us that the fall corrupted man completely, so that even his intellect is damaged and his heart totally depraved, we cannot develop an apologetic method that counts on the objectivity and goodness of humanity. By knowing sound doctrine thoroughly, therefore, we will possess more powerful intellectual arguments against unbelief.

Our doctrinal convictions begin with a faithful study of the Bible. We should move from the text of Scripture to our theological system, then to our apologetic methodology. This has the benefit of making us logically consistent, which is important since we aim to reveal the logical inconsistency and contradiction of the unbeliever's worldview. The more we know Scripture, the stronger our theological conclusions will be, which in turn will make our defense of the faith more robust.

The Doctrine of Scripture

The doctrine of Scripture is one of the most important doctrines to know in depth, since the Bible serves as our foundation for knowing what we know. The Bible is also the target of many attacks on Christianity, so the better we know how it was written, what it says about itself, its historical nature, and place in Christian theology, the better we will be able to defend all of the Christian faith.

What Is the Bible?

There are many ideas about what the Bible is. Some believe it is like many of the rest of sacred religious books from around the world—pious people's reflections on their experiences of the divine. Others believe the Bible is simply a collection of myths that some people mistakenly take to be true. The Christian view, however, is that the Bible is the revelation of God about himself and his divine plan to redeem the world. The Bible, then, is the very Word of God to his creatures for the purpose of redeeming them. Second Timothy 3:16 tells us that the words of Scripture are the very words of God breathed out by God himself. This is what we call the doctrine of *inspiration*. God the Holy Spirit moved human authors to write his words so that each word, and the final finished product, are exactly what God wanted to be written and without any errors. This is what we call the doctrine of *inerrancy*.

Because God is the ultimate author of Scripture, all his power and authority are invested in it. The Bible is not a dead book or an inert substance that has no power. Rather, the words of Scripture, being the very words of God, have incredible power to expose, convict, and transform the human heart (Heb. 4:12). Unbelievers often think that Christians merely follow the instructional teachings of a lifeless two-thousand-year-old book of facts and commandments. In reality, Christians follow the living God who has spoken through his Word, which is a living and powerful document. When we defend the Bible, we should do it with this in mind.

Our relationship to the Bible is not like reading instructions on assembling a bicycle, but rather is like reading a personal, handwritten invitation by the president of the United States to dine weekly with him at the White House. Such an invitation would contain some instructions, of course, but its primary intent would be to invite you into a relationship with a kind and powerful ruler who wants to invite you to serve him in a prestigious position. Even more, it is like receiving legal papers informing you that you have been adopted into a family who loves you and wants you to come home and be part of the family.

Sometimes unbelievers will fault Christians for believing in the Bible while missing this very point. Christians don't believe the Bible because they want to live with as many rules as possible. No, Christians believe the Bible because they have discovered that it lays out the path to a restored relationship to God. And the Bible goes further, clearly teaching how we can participate in God's great work of redemption in this life, and how we can have peace and joy for all eternity in the next life.

Another detail about the Bible many unbelievers don't know is that while it is a single book, it is also a collection of sixty-six books with a unified message. It is a library of books bound by a single theme of redemption. The Bible was written over the course of 1,400 years by more than forty authors, and yet is unified in its message. The Old Testament was written over a thousand-year span, and the manuscripts were carefully preserved by the Jewish people to ensure accuracy. The New Testament was written over a fifty-year span and was carefully preserved by the Christian church. (The reliability of the Bible will be covered in more detail in a later section.)

In addition, the books of the Bible are comprised of many writing styles, or *genres*. In the Old Testament these include law books (Genesis–Deuteronomy), history (Joshua–Esther), poetry and wisdom literature (Job–Song of Songs), and prophets (Isaiah–Malachi). In the New Testament we have the Gospels, or biographies (Matthew–John), history (Acts), epistles (Romans–Jude), and apocalyptic literature (Revelation). Each of these genres serves a different purpose in the unfolding story of redemption.

This is important, because unbelievers often know nothing about how the Bible came to be or about its various genres, let alone how to properly interpret them. They know that the Bible is old, but don't know much else about it, except perhaps that there are miraculous stories written in it. The Bible is actually an amazing piece of literature in its own right, in addition to being the revelation from God, so we can be rightly restored to him. One of our goals in apologetics is to get unbelievers to read the Bible for themselves. Countless people through the ages have been saved simply by reading the Bible for themselves.

How Did We Get the Bible?

The Bible did not fall from heaven as a finished product placed in the hands of men. Neither was it, like the claims of both Mormonism and Islam, translated from golden plates found in a hillside or cave. Rather, God communicated to human authors in various ways, and guided their writing so that what was written was what God wanted to reveal to them. While 2 Timothy 3:16 tells us what Scripture is, the clearest passage that describes this process is found in 2 Peter 1:16–21.

In this text we see that those human authors who wrote the books of the Bible did not do so on their own initiative (2 Pet. 1:19–21). They did not decide to sit down and write sacred texts. Rather, as the Holy Spirit moved in their hearts and minds, they wrote divine thoughts, mediated through their personalities and styles. The end result is Scripture that accurately communicates what God wanted to say, with humans as the instruments of God's revelation. The word translated "carried along" or "moved" is also used to describe the effect the wind has on sails. The wind blows into the sails, which moves the ship forward. Peter is saying that as the Holy Spirit initiated revelation to the authors of Scripture, they wrote under his influence and guidance.

One question often raised pertains to the reliability of the Bible after all these years. Many critics charge that we could not possibly know what the original words of Scripture were, because of errors in the copies. Two examples help dispel that notion. First, the Old Testament was carefully preserved by trained scribes in Israel whose main duty was to preserve the ancient texts. Their success in this is demonstrated in the discovery of the Dead Sea Scrolls in 1947 in Israel. Among the scrolls found was a copy of Isaiah that was dated to about 100 BC. Before this discovery, the oldest known copy of Isaiah dated back to 900 AD. The difference in the copies, then, was about 1,000 years apart. Scholars were amazed to find that these copies were virtually identical to each other, showing very little difference. The only differences were minor spelling mistakes that did not in any way affect the meaning of the text of Isaiah. And Jesus held people accountable to the words of the Old Testament, demonstrating his belief that they had been faithfully preserved down to his day.

The New Testament manuscripts are equally reliable. When we compare the almost 5,800 Greek manuscripts that date back to the second century AD, they are more than 95 percent identical to one another, and the remaining 5 percent of differences are spelling variations and simply errors made by later copyists that can be clearly identified as copy mistakes. None of these differences affect the teaching or doctrine of the Bible at all. In addition to Greek copies, we possess almost twenty thousand early copies of the New Testament in many other languages also, including Latin, Syriac, Coptic (from Egypt), Gothic, Armenian, Nubian (from Sudan), and many more. All of these show remarkable consistency over the centuries.

The conclusion to this is that the Bible is extremely reliable, even though parts of it are 3,500 years old. That means that when we confess that the Bible is our source of truth for doctrine and life, we can hold it confidently.

What Role Does the Bible Play in Christian Doctrine?

Since the time of the Reformation, Christians have summarized their beliefs about the Bible in four words. These attributes of Scripture form an acrostic, SCAN, which stands for sufficiency, clarity, authority, and necessity.

First, the *sufficiency* of Scripture means that the Bible contains everything we need to know for salvation and living in a way that pleases God (2 Pet. 1:3). Nothing needs to be added in order to make up for a lack in it. It is a finished, complete document that communicates all that Christians need to know about God in order to be rightly related to him and to live godly lives in this world (2 Tim. 3:16–17).

Sufficiency also means that Scripture is the final word from God (Heb. 1:1–2). Just as Jesus is the final revelation of God, and is the living Word of God, the Bible objectively declares all that God wants us to know about him. This is why nothing can be added or deleted from the Bible (Rev. 22:18–19). While tradition can help us understand how faithful Christians of the past have understood the Scripture, and gives us a pattern for faithful Christian living, the Bible is the final arbiter of truth.

Second, the *clarity* of Scripture means that the teaching of Scripture about salvation and godly living can be understood by all who seek to study it in belief. This does not mean that everything in Scripture is equally clear, for there are some parts that are difficult to comprehend. It does mean, however, that

God has not hidden the meaning of his revelation behind vague and esoteric language. Most of the Bible is written in rather plain, straightforward language. It is pictured as a lamp that lights one's path (Psalm 119:105), leading clearly to truth and understanding.

Clarity also means that we do not need a religious expert to interpret the Bible for us. Every Christian possesses the indwelling Holy Spirit, who leads us into truth (Jn. 16:13). This does not mean that we can determine the meaning of the Bible for ourselves, or that we don't need to build on the community of the church or theological understanding of Christians of the past; rather, it means that the Bible is not incomprehensible to us unless a priest or religious authority tells us what it means.

Third, the *authority* of Scripture means that the Bible is revelation from God himself, and that we are obligated to listen to it and obey it. Whatever the Bible speaks about is the truth, and it should arbitrate between competing truth claims. This does not mean that other human endeavors do not help us know our world, but if they contradict a clear statement in Scripture, the determination of truth lies with Scripture. The reason for this is that the Bible is the very Word of God, so it possesses the authority of God himself.

The authority of Scripture implies that it is also trustworthy, without error, and reliable. This has been challenged in countless ways by science, history, archaeology, philosophy, and others, but the Bible has always proven itself to stand the scrutiny of the human mind. Unbelievers want to elevate their own reason and authority over the Bible, but this has failed them every time. Whatever man considers to be wiser than God is shown to be foolishness (1 Cor. 1:18–21).

Fourth, the *necessity* of Scripture means that apart from God revealing himself to us, we could not know God. While many things about God can be known by *general* revelation—what can be seen in the created order (Rom. 1:19–20)—the Scriptures are necessary for us to know that Jesus died and rose again to save us. God is divine, perfect, and infinite. We are creaturely, fallen, and finite. God is so different from us that we would have no way of knowing him. But God condescended to reveal himself so that we might be restored to him. God has spoken to us in a way that is clear, translatable, objective, and able to be preserved.

If God had not revealed himself in the Bible, we could not possibly know all the story of redemption that he has worked on our behalf. Because he has given us his Word, we can know the full riches of his gift of salvation through Christ. The necessity of God's Word for salvation means that unless someone brings the Word of God to unbelievers they won't know how to be saved (Rom. 10:13–15).

Conclusion

In order for us to defend the Christian faith, we must know what the Bible teaches about itself, and what Christians have always believed about it. The Bible is the bedrock of all that we believe and serves as the foundation for all that we call knowledge. It is important that we firmly grasp the truth about Scripture, especially in light of the many misconceptions and challenges raised against its reliability.

In addition, it is important for Christians to read and know the Bible on a personal level. It does no good to defend the Christian faith, share the gospel, and proclaim the truth of the Bible if we are not daily reading and meditating on it ourselves.

The Bible is not a fact book to memorize; it is the revelation of the living God that is to be understood, believed, and lived. Only then will it have the transformative effect that it is meant to have. The Scriptures transform more than just our knowledge; they completely renovate our hearts and minds, our words and actions, and our very being.

This is one reason why earlier in this book we learned that one of the best ways to become a good apologist and evangelist is to know the Scriptures and sound doctrine thoroughly. When we eat, sleep, and breathe the Scriptures, our senses are sharpened to discern and refute arguments that are false and idolatrous (Heb. 5:11–14). The Holy Spirit uses our knowledge of the Scriptures to give our minds the sharp ability to know what to say at the right time. As you consider the role of the Bible in apologetics, it is my hope that you will become a thoroughly biblical apologist.

Chapter Twelve

Knowing What You Believe 2— The Doctrine of God

Now that we have established the authority of the Scriptures to reveal God to us, we move on to what God tells us about himself and ourselves. Sadly, the doctrine of God is one of the most ignored subjects for many Christians. The very God we are defending is virtually unknown to us. As we said in the previous chapter, theology is the study of God. But we don't study God like we study bacteria under a microscope. Rather, we study God as finite, fallen creatures learning about an infinitely greater being who has revealed himself to us for the purpose of relationship. We study God as desperate, needy people who receive a message of peace and blessing from a benevolent king who has showered us with grace upon grace.

Since there is limited space in this book, we can only touch on a few points about God and man. We will focus on the theological truths that serve as the foundation for our apologetic endeavors.

The Triunity of God

Most Asian religions, animism, and the ancient Greek, Roman, and Babylonian religions taught polytheism, the existence of many gods. Judaism, Islam, and Mormonism, on the other hand, teach that God is one without distinctions. The God of the Bible, Yahweh (Jehovah), on the other hand is both one and three. This is what we call the triunity of God, or the Trinity. This is one of the most difficult concepts to grasp for anyone, because there is nothing in our world to which we can compare this doctrine.

There is no human analogy that adequately pictures the relationship between God's oneness and threeness. Analogies such as the three states of water (liquid, gas, and solid) or the three parts of an egg (shell, white, and yolk, yet one egg) fail to properly picture the triunity of God. It is something we believe because Scripture teaches it, not because we can fully understand it. Because we are creaturely, finite and fallen, we should expect that some attributes of God will be beyond our ability to comprehend. Our minds are similar to a calculator, and God's nature is like a supercomputer operating system. We can't download and run the operating system because we simply do not have the capacity. If God did not exceed our ability to comprehend, how would he be worthy of our worship? Therefore, we accept the Bible's teaching on the Trinity and explore its depths as much as we can, but we realize that at some point our ability to comprehend it fully falls short.

For the purpose of this study, only a few points about God's triune nature will be emphasized here. First, God is equally three and one. He is not more one than he is three, and not more three than he is one. We speak of one essence in three persons and three persons in one essence. God as one thinks, feels, and knows as an individual being. Yet, each person of the Trinity has a unique consciousness. When Jesus cried out to the Father on the cross, he was not speaking to himself, but rather to the Father. Yet, both are God. All three persons of the Trinity are called God in the Scriptures, yet they are distinguished from one another.

The Father is called God (Rom. 1:7; 15:6; 1 Cor. 1:3; 8:6). The Son is called God (2 Pet. 1:1; Titus 2:13), calls himself God (Jn. 5:18), and accepts worship as God (Jn. 20:28–29). The Spirit is equated to God (Acts 5:3–4) and is the one who searches the mind of God (1 Cor. 2:10–11). Clearly, then, the Scriptures teach that each of the persons of the Trinity is God. Yet, God is one God. The unity of God was the foundation of Jewish religion, in contrast to the polytheistic religions of the nations around Israel (Deut. 6:4; Isa. 44:6–8). The New Testament likewise repeatedly emphasizes that there is only one God (Jn. 1:18; Eph. 4:6; 1 Cor. 8:6; 1 Tim. 2:5).

Some would say that the Trinity is a contradiction, but it is clearly not. A contradiction would be to say, "God is one and God is not one." The Christian doctrine of God, however, states that God is one and three, and his oneness and threeness are understood in different ways. God is one in essence, and three in person. These terms cannot be reversed. God is not three essences. That would make our understanding of God polytheistic—a belief in three gods. Rather, there is only one divine essence. Within the one divine essence are three persons—the Father, the Son, and the Holy Spirit.

This makes the Trinity a paradox, an *apparent* contradiction, not an actual contradiction. A paradox is something that is difficult, but not impossible, to reconcile logically and intellectually. Certainly, the Trinity is one of the most difficult doctrines that Christians believe; yet we do believe it, because the Bible teaches it.

One of the strengths of the Christian view of God is that it can answer the fundamental question of philosophy—the question of "the one and the many." The problem of the one and the many addresses the question of how existence (the one) relates to every individual thing that exists (the many). This is universally recognized as the most basic question with which philosophers wrestle. While there is no room here to develop this idea, we will simply note that in the triune God the one and the many exist in perfect harmony. In other words, God's being is the basis for an answer to philosophy's most pressing conundrum.

The Absolute Personality of God

Second, God is the absolute, personal God. The God that Christians trust and defend is a personal God—that is, he possesses rationality and self-consciousness. This is apparent in that God does things that persons do. He creates, speaks, leads, judges, gives, loves, controls, punishes, wills, and many other actions. He can be pleased, grieved, angered, betrayed, saddened, and appeased. God relates to us as a person who understands, communicates, and responds to us. God is not a force or an idea, but a personal God who is intent on pursuing those made in his image to restore relationship with him. So each member of the Godhead is personal, and the triune God is also personal. These concepts are beyond our understanding, but they are comforting in that we know that there is no impersonal aspect of God. God is never a mere force or "thing." He is fully personal and relates to us in a personal way.

Third, the Christian God is absolute. He is all-powerful, all-knowing, and everywhere at once. He does not share power with anyone else. He is the only God in the universe, and all authority resides in him. There is no yin-yang relationship between God and Satan. There are no equally dark and light sides of the force. God alone is uncreated, eternally God, and everything else that exists is created, finite, and fallen.

The attributes of personal and absolute stand in sharp contrast to the impersonal gods of philosophy, Islam, Buddhism, and deism. These belief systems hold to a God who is not much different than the law of gravity—very powerful, but not a being to whom one relates. On the other hand, many religions have personal gods who are not absolute. The Greek, Roman, and Egyptian pantheon of gods are a good example, as are the 330 million gods of Hinduism, and the spirit beings of Asian religions and tribal religions. All false gods are either personal or absolute, but not both. Only the Christian God is personal and absolute.

The Aseity of God

Finally, God is *a se*. Aseity means that God is self-existing, all-sufficient, and supreme. God needs nothing outside himself. Unlike the pagan gods, the Christian God does not need a single thing from us. Paul made this a central point of his address to the philosophers in Athens in Acts 17. In pagan religion the people needed the gods and the gods needed the people. Paul informs his hearers that the true God needs nothing from us. On the contrary, we need everything from him. "In him we live and move and have our being" (17:28).

God did not need to create the world, nor did he have to save us. He does not need us to become fully God, as some would argue. We need him for everything, including the upholding of the entire universe (Col. 1:15–20). Before creation the persons of the Trinity were in eternal, perfect, personal, loving fellowship with one another. There was nothing lacking or incomplete. The fact that God created a world that he knew would rebel against him and eternally chose to save unworthy sinners by the death of the Son shows that at his essence, God gives and loves for the good of others and for his glory. This is the Christian God we seek to share and defend in our apologetic efforts.

It is important, therefore, that when Christians defend God, they have these distinctive attributes of God in mind, so they are not tricked into trying to defend a God in which they don't, in fact, believe. For example, if an unbeliever says, "I can't believe in a God who would create the world and walk away while it falls apart," our response would be something like, "I don't believe in that kind of God either." We don't want to defend a distortion of God as revealed in Scripture, but rather, the true God of Scripture.

Conclusion

Not only is the truth of God important for apologetics, but it is also important for the fullness of Christian faith. That is, these truths of God's triune nature and personality are precious to believers because they show us who God is. As a result, we come to God more truly and that brings us closer to him. Knowing someone in great detail makes for a stronger relationship. The more we know God through the Scriptures, the more our relationship will strengthen our apologetic efforts. In the next chapter we will look at one more doctrine—the doctrine of man and his fall into sin.

Chapter Thirteen

Knowing What You Believe 3—
The Doctrines of Man and Sin

W e are unique from all the rest of creation by being made in the image of God. We are not like animals or angels because we were created to reflect the glory and image of God. Humans alone in creation are made in God's image and likeness. This partly explains why all people are without excuse before God—their very purpose is to be in relation to God. To deny God when we are designed to reflect his glory is to rebel against everything that we are. To deny the existence of God is to deny our very humanity.

For the sake of brevity, we can only touch on a few points about man and sin. We will once again focus on the theological truths that serve as the foundation for our apologetic endeavors.

Man and Sin

The view that a particular religion or worldview has about human beings tells a lot about important issues, such as the meaning and purpose of life, human dignity, what is wrong with the world, and the nature of right and wrong. In many worldviews, man is nothing more than a product of the blind force of evolution. This makes him an accident of nature, since there can be no intelligence in the universe. In this view, man is nothing more than an animal, and no purpose or meaning can be derived from random forces. This view, however, makes human dignity and ethics impossible to argue. If man is just an animal, then violence, disease, and calamity are just the nature of life.

In other views, such as New Age religion, Hinduism, and most of the Asian religions, man is divine and a spawn of the gods. Man finds his dignity in having a spark of the divine within himself, or else he is just as much god as anything else. One of the problems with this view, however, is that these supposedly divine humans commit evil acts. If a divine being does evil, what makes it evil? And considering the amount of evil in the world, what good does the divine do in the world? These questions cannot be answered in a meaningful way if everything is equally divine.

The biblical view of man, however, provides answers to the most pressing questions of humanity, such as where did I come from, why am I here, what is wrong with the world, who am I, what is my purpose, and where am I going?

As with the doctrine of the Trinity, only a few areas can be addressed here. First, man is created in the image of God. The Bible teaches that man is a special creation of God, different from the animals by virtue of being made in God's image (Gen. 1:26–27). In this sense, man is greater than the angels who do not bear the image of God. Because man is made in God's image, he bears intrinsic value and dignity, apart from anything he does. This dignity is so basic that because of the image of God, to murder is to commit a crime that strikes against God himself. As a result, God demands that the life of the murderer be taken by proper authorities, to demonstrate the heinous nature of such an act (Gen. 9:6).

The image of God is never explicitly explained in Scripture, but most theologians agree that it pertains to rationality, a sense of right and wrong, and the implanted knowledge of God. These inherent qualities demonstrate that God is a personal, moral being who has revealed himself to all people. Our calling as human beings is to know God through Christ, live a life marked by wisdom and obedience to God, and share the good news of Jesus Christ, which is the wisdom of God. This feature of humanity—being made in God's image—is the key to human identity and understanding our place in God's world.

The image of God in man also means that God is the original and we are the copy. God is the eternal I AM, and we are an icon, or picture, that reflects the glory of the I AM. The reflection is not praised or worshiped; rather, the reality is worshiped. Resuming the analogy from earlier in this book, if a soldier has a picture of his wife with him on the battlefield, he stares at her image to remind him of her beauty. But the picture can fade and be wrinkled in a day. When he returns to her, he does not stare at the picture anymore, but gazes upon the beauty of his wife, who is now right in front of him. In the same way, we are to so reflect the glory of God that people want to worship God when they see our lives.

Second, man is different from God. Many world religions, especially the Asian religions, have a monistic view of the world. That is, they believe that all things that exist are the same at the core. All things participate in *being*, and God or the gods possess more being than we creatures. The goal in these religions is either to erase the distinctions between man and the gods, or to be swallowed up into the Great Divine and cease to exist.

Regardless of the details, man is not at all or not much different in his essence than God. This view can be depicted as follows:

Being

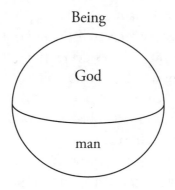

The Christian view of God is quite different, in contrast. We believe in what is called the Creator/creature distinction (CCD). The CCD teaches that God is wholly other than us. God is infinite, holy, and divine. In contrast we are finite, fallen, and creaturely. God has always been God and always will be God. We are creaturely (created beings), and will always be creaturely, even when we obtain our glorified bodies in eternity.

Since we are finite, fallen, and creaturely, we could know nothing about the infinite, holy, divine God unless he revealed himself to us. And this is what makes the Christian God unique. God not only tells us who he is, but he continually comes down to us to reveal himself. We call this the condescension of God. All through the Bible God stoops down to his creation to show and tell us who he is and how we can be reconciled to him. In addition to his revelation, God providentially guides all things by his sovereign power. These two things—revelation and providence—are how we as creatures know the triune God.

The Christian view can be depicted as follows:

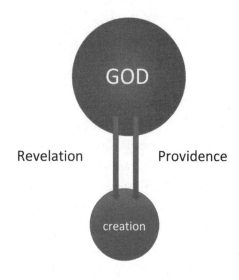

In Genesis 1:2 we are told that the Holy Spirit was hovering over the waters as God was creating. In Genesis 3:8 God comes down to confront Adam and Eve about eating the forbidden fruit. In Genesis 7:16 God closes the door of the ark himself. In Genesis 32:24–32 God wrestles with Jacob and gives him a new name. In Exodus 3:7–8 God comes down to see the suffering of his people before he leads them out of Egypt. Over and over throughout the Bible God comes down to his people, protecting them, speaking with them, rescuing them. This culminates in the incarnation of the Son of God adding a human nature to his eternal divine nature with the birth of Jesus. In this ultimate sense God has come down and revealed himself and reconciled us to God.

The CCD reminds us that God is not like us, and that his ways are not our ways (Isa. 55:8–9). One of the distinctions of

Christianity is that we do not make images of God, because those who do invariably make idols in the likeness of other created things (Rom. 1:22–23). But God is so different than us that he forbids the making of idols because they cannot represent him. However, God has revealed himself to us in his Word and through his Son. This means that we can know him, because he has chosen to reveal himself to us.

Some, such as agnostics, like to argue that even if God exists, we can't know anything about him. Such would be true, if it weren't for the fact that God has revealed himself to us. This is why a clear doctrine of Scripture is so important for Christians. We are able to escape ignorance by acknowledging the Bible as God's Word to us.

Third, man was designed to represent God on earth. Not only are human beings made in the image of God, but also from the beginning man was given purpose through the tasks given to him in the garden of Eden. Genesis 1:28–30 reminds us that man was to rule over the earth and cultivate it. That is, Adam and Eve were to develop all the natural resources on earth for their enjoyment, pleasure, and comfort. Everything we have in our modern world today—the Hubble Space Telescope, computers, robotic surgery, skyscrapers—was in the ground when Adam and Eve were created. God gave man the commission to cultivate the potential of the earth. This is a noble calling!

Fourth, because of sin, man is completely fallen. In contrast to many worldviews and religions, Christianity believes that man is fallen and his heart is corrupt. Since the fall into sin, every person is born with a depraved heart that will not choose God apart from the Holy Spirit's supernatural drawing to Christ (Rom. 3:10–18; Jn. 14:6; 6:44). In the garden of Eden, Adam and Eve tried to do without God in every respect. By rejecting

God's evaluation of the Tree of the Knowledge of Good and Evil, they asserted their right to interpret the world as they saw fit. In the case of the forbidden fruit Eve determined that it was "good" for food, even though God declared it to be spiritually and physically poisonous.

The motivation for Eve's disobedience, however, was not simply to try a new flavor of fruit, but to transcend her humanity to become divine, as the serpent had promised her (Gen. 3:5). In other words, Eve wanted to escape her creaturely limits and become like God—infinite and divine. This was all a lie, however, and her actions resulted in death. Many false religions and worldviews are based on a desire to become divine, or to escape death like God. What they promise, however, can never come true. Humans will always be created beings, finite and limited.

In eating the fruit Adam and Eve also attempted to decide for themselves what is right and wrong. They tried to establish their own ethics in rebellion of God's declaration of right and wrong. Here is another common aspect of non-Christian belief systems: They want to reject God's laws and establish their own. These false ethical standards often lead to a removal of any restraint whatsoever, which leads to violence, abuse, and anarchy. We see this most clearly in the days of Noah (Gen. 6:5, 11–12), the time of the judges (Judg. 17:6; 21:25), and the last days predicted in the New Testament (2 Tim. 3:1–9).

The result of the fall is that every one of natural man's intellectual and spiritual functions operates wrongly. Man's thinking is now slanted away from God in rebellion and ignorance (Eph. 4:17–19). Man is not objective, because his sinful, evil heart turns away from God, truth, beauty, and goodness, and seeks to satisfy self. The result is that man embraces lies, ugliness, and evil. He loves the darkness of sin rather than the light of truth (Jn. 3:19–21; Rom. 1:25).

Cornelius Van Til used two pictures to illustrate this truth. Imagine a woodworker who sets his table saw to exact measurements to cut boards at a right angle. He leaves the workshop for a few minutes to get the wood, and while he is gone his ten-year-old son enters the room and changes the angle of the saw. Every board that the woodworker cuts after that will be wrong and will be damaged. In the same way God created us holy and perfect, with our intellect, emotions, and will operating rightly. After the fall, these faculties are now damaged, and while they resemble the original design, they are damaged and do not function properly.

Van Til's second illustration helps us understand the unbeliever's bias against God and the truth. Imagine yellow-lensed goggles glued to the face of the unbeliever. Everything he sees now has a yellow hue. He cannot see colors correctly because of these goggles. Yet he insists he is wearing no goggles and sees colors correctly. In the same way, the fall has distorted man's intellectual understanding, and he cannot see truthfully until the Holy Spirit removes the goggles in salvation. It takes the regeneration of man's reason to correct the damage done by the fall. When a person is saved, the Holy Spirit replaces his unbelieving heart of stone with a "heart of flesh" that now functions properly (Ezek. 11:19–21; 36:26–27). He takes away spiritual blindness and replaces it with sight (Jn. 9:39).

Conclusion

Having a biblical understanding of God and man provides many powerful avenues for apologetics. We avoid defending concepts we don't believe. We tap into the powerful truths of the wisdom and power of God (1 Cor. 1:24). The more we know the Scriptures and sound doctrine, the more weapons we possess in the war of ideas. We are able to more effectively destroy arguments and pull down strongholds of unbelief (2 Cor. 10:3–5). Knowing what we believe is the best foundation for apologetics and evangelism, because it gives us the ability to answer unbelief from any direction.

Conclusion

You may have reached this point in the book and are surprised to suddenly see the conclusion. Where are all the evidences? Where are the arguments for the existence of God? Where are the "Top 10 objections raised against the Christian faith"? When do we learn how to engage Muslims, Hindus, and Zoroastrians?

These are all important, but to answer those questions adequately would require this book to be doubled or tripled in size. Furthermore, there are already dozens of good books that engage those questions and many more in great detail. I list almost one hundred good resources in the Bibliography of Suggested Resources, arranged by topic.

The reason I don't try to answer those and other questions in this book is twofold. First, if you could learn adequate answers for dozens of objections that are commonly raised against the Christian faith, but don't know how to deploy them effectively, they are practically useless. It would be the equivalent of someone knowing every possible fact about the human body, but never going to medical school to learn how to treat the sick and injured. While I am all for reading, studying, and learning apologetics as thoroughly as possible, if you can't engage unbelievers effectively and winsomely in gospel conversations, you may do more harm than good. There are, unfortunately, a growing number of Christians who are very knowledgeable about Christianity, philosophy, science, and other related fields, but are relational bulldozers when they try to engage unbelievers. It does no good to acquire knowledge if we do not also possess the love and skill with which to deploy it.

I hope this book has helped you develop a framework for engaging any person you meet. You can see that our proposed strategy is not formulaic, but responsive and relational, allowing you to get to the heart of the unbeliever's resistance to the gospel in a natural way. Because it is not a formula, it takes time and practice to learn well. My hope is that you will be encouraged by this approach and will feel confident to actually practice the kind of evangelism about which Christians speak so frequently but don't do.

Second, if you wait until you have studied apologetics for years and feel fully prepared to answer any question that may come your way, you will never actually share your faith. You will never fulfill the call of 1 Peter 3:15–16, which goes beyond the preparation to the actual defending, or answering. I know this from personal experience. Do you remember the opening story of my engagement with Karen and Bill? That encounter took place in the first few weeks of my introduction to the method we have learned in this book. And yet, almost fifteen years later, still I pass up opportunities to engage unbelievers with the gospel sometimes because I worry that they might ask me a question I don't know how to answer. What if they throw existentialism or Shinto at me? What if they ask me something about the Egyptian myth of Horus and Osiris and its supposed similarities to the person of Jesus? What if they tell me that they have found more peace and hope since they abandoned Christianity? The list goes on and on.

One of the challenges of learning apologetics without simultaneously practicing it is that you can often find yourself paralyzed into inaction. The more you study apologetics, the more you see that an almost infinite number of questions or objections can be raised. You can begin to shrink back out of a fear that will only grow worse over time. Of course, we want to be ever-growing in our understanding of the Christian faith and various objections against the gospel, but you must know that there will never come a time that you will gain confidence solely through the accumulation of knowledge.

The problem with mastery without practice is that it tempts us to trust ourselves and not the Holy Spirit and the power of the message itself. Paul reminds us in 1 Corinthians 1:23–25 that the message of Christ crucified is the power of God and the wisdom of God:

> [B]ut we preach Christ crucified, a stumbling block to Jews and folly to Gentiles, but to those who are called, both Jews and Greeks, Christ the power of God and the wisdom of God. For the foolishness of God is wiser than men, and the weakness of God is stronger than men.

Paul continues by reminding us that even when he felt inadequate and without eloquence, he knew the gospel would go forth in power because it did not depend on him, but God.

> And I was with you in weakness and in fear and much trembling, and my speech and my message were not in plausible words of wisdom, but in demonstration of the Spirit and of power, so that your faith might

> not rest in the wisdom of men but in the power of
> God. (1 Cor. 2:3–5)

I need to learn to trust the gospel message above my own mastery of apologetics. If I do, I will be more likely to step out in faith to engage others in conversation. My hope and prayer as you finish this book is that you will immediately begin to put into practice what you have learned. Move past your fears and sense of inadequacy and engage someone with the gospel this week. Pray fervently that God will give you wisdom and power, and see if you do not experience the thrill and joy of participating in God's great work of saving people through Christ!

End Notes

1. J. P. Louw and Eugene A. Nida, *Greek-English Lexicon of the New Testament: Based on Semantic Domains* (New York: United Bible Societies, 1988).

2. Cornelius Van Til, *Christian Apologetics,* 2nd ed. Ed. by William Edgar (Phillipsburg, NJ: P&R Publishers, 2003), 17.

3. W. Edgar, "Christian Apologetics for a New Century: Where We Have Come From, Where We Are Going," in *New Dictionary of Christian Apologetics* (Downers Grove, IL: InterVarsity Press, 2006), 3.

4. See K. Scott Oliphint, *Covenantal Apologetics* (Phillipsburg, NJ: P&R Publishers, 2013), 38–39, for an explanation of the history of the term presuppositional and his preference for the label *covenantal.*

5. Abraham Kuyper, *Lectures on Calvinism* (Grand Rapids: Eerdmans, 1943), 11.

6. Oliphint, *Covenantal Apologetics,* 233.

7. Peter van Inwagen, *Metaphysics,* 2nd ed., Dimension of Philosophy Series (Boulder, CO: Westview, 2002), 12.

8. This section is a distillation of teaching I first heard in Scott Oliphint's apologetics class at Westminster Theological Seminary.

9. Adapted from Os Guiness, *Fool's Talk: Recovering the Art of Christian Persuasion* (Downers Grove, IL: InterVarsity Press, 2015), 18.

10. See Greg Bahnsen, *Always Ready: Directions for Defending the Faith* (Nacogdoches, TX: Covenant Media Press, 1995), x111–12.

11. Bahnsen, "Ready to Reason," Answers in Genesis, February 11, 2009, https://answersingenesis.org/apologetics/ready-to-reason.

12. Thomas Nagel, *The Last Word* (New York: Oxford University Press, 1997), 130–31.

13. G. K. Beale, *We Become What We Worship: A Biblical Theology of Idolatry* (Downers Grove, IL: InterVarsity Press, 2008), 17.

14. Timothy Keller, *Counterfeit Gods: The Empty Promises of Money, Sex, and Power, and the Only Hope That Matters* (New York: Dutton, 2009), xviii.

15. David Foster Wallace, "This Is Water" (Full Transcript and Audio), Farnam Street, https://fs.blog/2012/04/david-foster-wallace-this-is-water. The wording has been slightly altered to clarify and/or provide context.

16. Laurence J. Peter, (1977). *Peter's Quotations: Ideas for Our Times* (New York: William Morrow), p. 44.

17. G. K. Chesterton, "The Oracle of the Dog," in *The Complete Father Brown Stories* (Hertfordshire: Wordsworth Classics, 2006), 394-5.

18. Guinness, *Fool's Talk*, 53.

19. Bart D. Ehrman, *Did Jesus Exist? The Historical Argument for Jesus of Nazareth* (New York: HarperOne, 2012).

20. C. S. Lewis, *Mere Christianity* (New York: Macmillan, 1984), 55–56.

21. Lewis, "We were made for another world," C. S. Lewis Institute, http://www.cslewisinstitute.org/webfm_send/4509.

22. Rosaria Butterfield, *Secret Thoughts of an Unlikely Convert: An English Professor's Journey Into Christian Faith* (Crown and Covenant, 2012).

23. Quoted in Charles Taylor, *A Secular Age* (Cambridge, MA: Belknap, 2007), 596.

24. Gordon Clark, *Logic* (Unicoi, TN: Trinity Foundation, 1988),1

25. Adapted from Ibid.

26. Victor J. Stenger, "Quotable Quote," GoodReads, https://www.goodreads.com/quotes/282295-science-flies-you-to-the-moon-religion-flies-you-into.

Bibliography of Suggested Resources

Basic Apologetics

Nathan Busenitz, *Reasons We Believe: 50 Lines of Evidence that Confirm the Christian Faith* (Crossway, 2008)

Joshua Chatraw and Mark Allen, *Apologetics at the Cross* (Zondervan, 2018)

Os Guinness, *Fool's Talk: Recovering the Art of Christian Persuasion* (IVP, 2015)

Greg Koukl, *Tactics: A Game Plan for Discussing Your Christian Convictions* (Zondervan, 2009)

Greg Koukl, *The Story of Reality* (Zondervan, 2017)

C. S. Lewis, *Mere Christianity* (Harper, 2001)

K. Scott Oliphint, *The Battle Belongs to the Lord: The Power of Scripture for Defending Our Faith* (P&R, 2003)

K. Scott Oliphint, *Know Why You Believe* (Zondervan, 2017)

James Sire, *Why Good Arguments Often Fail: Making A More Persuasive Case for Christ* (IVP, 2006)

J. Warner Wallace, *Cold-Case Christianity: A Homicide Detective Investigates the Claims of the Gospels* (Cook, 2013)

J. Warner Wallace, *God's Crime Scene: The Evidence for a Divinely Created Universe* (David C. Cook, 2015)

J. Warner Wallace, *Forensic Faith: A Case for a More Reasonable, Evidential Christian Faith* (David C. Cook, 2017)

Atheism/Skepticism

John Frame, *Christianity Considered: A Guide for Skeptics and Seekers* (Lexham, 2018)

Timothy Keller, *The Reason for God: Belief in an Age of Skepticism* (Dutton, 2008)

Timothy Keller, *Making Sense of God: An Invitation to the Skeptical* (Viking, 2016)

Andreas Köstenberger, Darrell Bock, and Josh Chatraw, *Truth in a Culture of Doubt* (B&H, 2014)

John Lennox, *Gunning for God: Why the New Atheists Are Missing the Target* (Lion, 2011)

John Lennox, *Miracles: Is Belief in the Supernatural Irrational?* (Veritas, 2013)

Nancy Pearcey, *Finding Truth: 5 Principles for Unmasking Atheism, Secularism, and Other God Substitutes* (David C. Cook, 2015)

Mitch Stokes, *How to Be an Atheist: Why Many Skeptics Are Not Skeptical Enough* (Crossway, 2016)

Mitch Stokes, *A Shot of Faith to the Head: Be a Confident Believer in an Age of Cranky Atheists* (Thomas Nelson, 2012)

Ravi Zacharias, *The End of Reason: A Response to the New Atheists* (Zondervan, 2008)

The Reliability of Scripture

Craig Blomberg, *Can We Still Believe the Bible?* (Brazos, 2014)

Craig Blomberg, *The Historical Reliability of the New Testament* (B&H, 2016)

Kevin DeYoung, *Taking God at His Word: Why the Bible is Knowable, Necessary, and Enough* (Crossway, 2014)

Michael J. Kruger, *Canon Revisited: Establishing the Authority and Origins of the New Testament Books* (Crossway, 2012)

Michael Licona, *Why Are There Differences in the Gospels? What We Can Learn about Ancient Biography* (Oxford, 2016)

Vern Poythress, *Inerrancy and Worldview: Answering Modern Challenges to the Bible* (Crossway, 2012)

Peter J. Williams, *Can We Trust the Gospels?* (Crossway, 2018)

The Person, Death, and Resurrection of Jesus

Richard Bauckham, *Jesus and the Eyewitnesses: The Gospels as Eyewitness Testimony* (Eerdmans, 2017)

Michael F. Bird, et al., *How God Became Jesus: The Real Origins of Belief in Jesus' Divine Nature* (Zondervan, 2014)

Jonathan K. Dodson and Brad Watson, *Raised? Finding Jesus by Doubting the Resurrection* (Zondervan, 2014)

Gary Habermas and Michael Licona, *The Case for the Resurrection of Jesus* (Kregel, 2004)

N. T. Wright, *The Resurrection of the Son of God* (Fortress, 2003)

Old Testament Issues in Apologetics

John Currid, *Against the Gods: The Polemical Theology of the Old Testament* (Crossway, 2013)

James K. Hoffmeier and Dennis R. Magary, eds. *Do Historical Matters Matter to Faith?* (Crossway, 2012)

David T. Lamb, *God Behaving Badly: Is the God of the Old Testament Angry, Sexist and Racist?* (IVP, 2011)

Miscellaneous

Rosaria Butterfield, *The Gospel Comes with a House Key* (Crossway, 2018)

Vern Poythress, *In the Beginning Was the Word: Language: A God-Centered Approach* (Crossway, 2009)

Vern Poythress, *Redeeming Sociology: A God-Centered Approach* (Crossway, 2011)

Vern Poythress, *Redeeming Mathematics: A God-Centered Approach* (Crossway, 2015)

Islam

Nabeel Qureshi, *Seeking Allah, Finding Jesus* (Zondervan, 2014)

Nabeel Qureshi, *Answering Jihad: A Better Way Forward* (Zondervan, 2015)

Nabeel Qureshi, *No God but One: Allah or Jesus?* (Zondervan, 2016)

James R. White, *What Every Christian Needs to Know About the Qur'an* (Bethany House, 2013)

Anees Zaka and Diane Coleman, *The Truth about Islam: The Noble Qur'an's Teachings in Light of the Holy Bible* (P&R, 2004)

Truth and Tolerance

D. A. Carson, *The Intolerance of Tolerance* (Eerdmans, 2012)

Stewart Kelly, *Truth Considered and Applied: Examining Postmodernism, History, and Christian Faith* (B&H, 2011)

Andreas Köstenberger, ed. *Whatever Happened to Truth?* (Crossway, 2012)

Abdu Murray, *Saving Truth: Finding Meaning and Clarity in a Post-Truth World* (Zondervan, 2018)

James Sire, *Why Should Anyone Believe Anything at All?* (IVP, 1994)

Sexuality

Sam Allberry, *Is God Anti-Gay?* (The Good Book Company, 2013)

Rosaria Butterfield, *Secret Thoughts of an Unlikely Convert: An English Professor's Journey into Christian Faith* (Crown and Covenant, 2012)

Rosaria Butterfield, *Openness Unhindered: Further Thoughts of an Unlikely Convert* (Crown and Covenant, 2012)

Joe Dallas, *When Homosexuality Hits Home: What to Do When a Loved One Says "I'm Gay"* (Harvest, 2015)

Kevin DeYoung, *What Does the Bible Really Teach about Homosexuality?* (Crossway, 2015).

Robert Gagnon, *The Bible and Homosexual Practice* (Abingdon, 2002)

Peter Hubbard, *Love into Light: The Gospel, the Homosexual, and the Church* (Ambassador International, 2013)

Dennis Jernigan, *Sing Over Me: An Autobiography* (Innova Publishing, 2014)

Nancy R. Pearcey, *Love Thy Body: Answering Hard Questions about Life and Sexuality* (Baker, 2017)

Glenn T. Stanton, *Loving My (LGBT) Neighbor: Being Friends in Grace and Truth* (Moody, 2014)

Andrew Walker, *God and the Transgender Debate* (The Good Book Company, 2017)

Science

Michael Behe, *Darwin Devolves: The New Science about DNA That Challenges Evolution* (HarperOne: 2019)

John Lennox, *Against the Flow: The Inspiration of Daniel in an Age of Relativism* (Monarch, 2015)

John Lennox, *God's Undertaker: Has Science Buried God?* (Lion, 2011)

John Lennox, *God and Stephen Hawking: Whose Design Is It Anyway?* (Lion, 2011)

John Lennox, *Can Science Explain Everything?* (The Good Book Company, 2019)

John Lennox, *Seven Days that Divide the World: The Beginning According to Genesis and Science* (Zondervan, 2011)

Stephen C. Meyer, *Darwin's Doubt: The Explosive Origin of Animal Life and the Case for Intelligent Design* (HarperOne, 2014)

J. P. Moreland, *Scientism and Secularism* (Crossway, 2018)

Vern Poythress, *Redeeming Science: A God-Centered Approach* (Crossway, 2006)

Evangelism and Apologetics

Jerram Barrs, *Learning Evangelism from Jesus* (Crossway, 2009)

Kevin Harney, *Organic Outreach for Ordinary People: Sharing Good News Naturally* (Zondervan, 2009)

Timothy Keller, *Encounters with Jesus: Unexpected Answers to Life's Biggest Questions* (Riverhead, 2013)

Will Metzger, *Tell the Truth: The Whole Gospel Wholly by Grace* (IVP, 2013)

Evil and Suffering

D. A. Carson, *How Long, O Lord? Reflection on Suffering and Evil* (IVP, 1990)

Jeremy Evans, *The Problem of Evil: The Challenge to Essential Christian Beliefs* (B&H, 2013)

John Feinberg, *The Many Faces of Evil* (Crossway, 2004)

C. S. Lewis, *The Problem of Pain* (HarperOne, 2002)

Worldview

James Anderson, *What's Your Worldview* (Crossway, 2014)

Tawa Anderson, W. Michael Clark, and David Naugle, *An Introduction to Christian Worldview* (IVP, 2017)

J. Mark Bertrand, *Rethinking Worldview: Learning to Think, Live, and Speak in This World* (Crossway, 2007)

Peter Jones, *The Other Worldview: Exposing Christianity's Greatest Threat* (Kirkdale, 2015)

James Sire, *Naming the Elephant: Worldview as a Concept* (IVP, 2004)

Albert M. Wolters, *Creation Regained: Biblical Basics for a Reformational Worldview*, 2nd ed. (Eerdmans, 2005)

Websites

Alpha and Omega Ministries: www.aomin.org

Answers in Genesis: www.answersingenesis.org

Apologetics 315: www.apologetics315.com

Christian Apologetics and Research Ministry: www.carm.org

The Discovery Institute: www.discovery.org

Probe: www.probe.org

Ratio Christi (Campus Apologetics Alliance): www.ratiochristi.org

Reasonable Faith: www.reasonablefaith.org

Mary Jo Sharp (Confident Christianity): www.maryjosharp.com

Stand to Reason: www.str.org

Ravi Zacharias International Ministries: www.rzim.org

Contact the Author

To contact Dr. Mark Farnham:

Email: apologeticsforthechurch@gmail.com

Website: www.apologeticsforthechurch.org

Facebook: https://www.facebook.com/mark.farnham.792

Twitter: https://twitter.com/proffarnham

Instagram: https://www.instagram.com/everybelieverconfident

Podcast: http://ap4c.buzzsprout.com